Country Girl

MEMOIRS OF A WEST TEXAS HOMECOMING QUEEN

KC Paper Co.
Walden, NY

Billie John Grable Jurlina

COUNTRY GIRL
published by *KC* Paper Co.

Manufacturing by Lulu.com
Cover design by Katherine A. Clark

KC Paper Co.
2522 State Route 208
Walden, NY 12586
KCPaperCompany.com

Printed in the United States of America

My father, John Francis Grable, was born on 4 March 1880 on William Riley (Bill) Smith's place in Bethesda, Parker County, Texas. He was the fourth of twelve children born to Virgil Lee Grable and Jane Cranfill. My father told me that his father was a very religious man and would pray for an hour sometimes before meals (I bet the food got cold.). His father was quite stern and a very severe disciplinarian.

When working in the fields with his four oldest sons, Virgil Lee would often stop the team and walk back to where the boys were hoeing and use the horsewhip on them. The boys, as teenagers, decided they had had enough of this treatment and the next time their father tried this, they would relieve him of the whip. Of course they all had to leave home after going against their father. My father moved in with his mother's parents, Isom and Sarah Torksey (Copeland) Cranfill. Isom owned the Whitt, Texas Bank and was quite a wealthy man for that day and time. I guess he should have been since he charged 25% interest most of the time. Isom had a reputation of helping people in need in spite of charging high interest. He and Sarah were devout members of the Disciples of Christ Church.

Willie Laura Vick, my mother, was born on 6 October 1887 in Ruston, Lincoln Parish, Louisiana. She was the youngest of seven daughters born to Nathan Monroe Vick and Mary Elizabeth Lopp. The two who died as infants were not named. (The names and birth order appear in Appendix A.)

Both of my parents grew up in the Whitt, Texas area. When they made the decision to marry, my mother was 15 and my father was 22. They were wed on 11 November 1902. My brother, John Aaron, was born 5 December 1904 in Whitt, Parker County, Texas. My sister, Mabel Louise, was born l September 1909 in Whitt, Parker County, Texas. (See copies of their birth certificates in Appendix B)

I was born in the Hamilton Hospital (named for Dr. George B. Hamilton, the doctor who delivered me) in Olney, Young County, Texas on September 28, 1924. Upon my birth, my mother went into convulsions and almost died. Since the hospital had no nursery, I was put in a dresser drawer in my mother's room. My brother, John Aaron (age 20), and my sister, Mabel Louise (age 15), named me Billie John after both my father (John) and my mother (Willie). At first I disliked my name very much because I wanted it to be more feminine, but in time I decided it was kind of neat to have an unusual name. (My birth certificate is in Appendix B.) This photograph is of our family when I was nine months old. Daddy is looking a little cross because the photographer told my mother to stand behind her father. I guess this made daddy feel older than he was.

My parents moved to Throckmorton County in 1917 after purchasing a farm consisting of 480 acres. Just before their move, my dad had been in the grocery and dry goods business with my grandfather, Nathan Monroe Vick. My dad ran the store while my Grandfather Vick ran a freight business. He hauled freight using a team of mules and a wagon between Weatherford and Whitt because there was no train. My parents made trips to Dallas where they bought dry goods and ready to wear clothing wholesale from Sanger Brothers. (Sanger's sold to Federated a few years ago and was renamed Foley's.) Today it is called Macy's. According to accounts from the family, the Vick-Grable business in Whitt was quite lucrative.

When my grandmother, Jane Cranfill, was eighteen she was still living with her parents in Authon, Parker County, Texas. Jane was in her upstairs bedroom watching her brother, Linn, (age 14) trying to catch his pony. She saw some Indians catch him and either shoot or scalp him. I have heard the story told both ways. It must have been a very sad time for them. Apparently that was the last reported killing by Cherokee Indians in that area.

(Left to right) Top Row: Sons of Virgil & Jane: Victor Grable, Isom G. Grable, Jesse Grable, John F. Grable, Clarence Grable & Robert Grable #7 Harry Cranfill, Pat Cranfill, Silas Cranfill, John Cranfill (sons of J.B. & Belle) Center Row: The 3 young Grables: Frank & Mary and Milton Cranfill (son of J.B. & Belle) Front Row: Virgil Grable, dtr. Florence, wife, Jane (Cranfill), Jane's father, Isom Cranfill & mother, Sarah Torksey (Copeland) Cranfill, Jane's brother J.B. Cranfill and his wife, Belle- J.B. & Belle's two young children: Leslie & Torksey

The Isom Cranfill family and the Wilson Grable family (pictures on opposite page) came to Texas from Kentucky by wagon train in 1870. They bought land in the Authon, Parker County area that is just a few miles from both Whitt and Bethesda and about 15 miles northwest of Weatherford. My great-grandfather Grable donated land and was responsible for building the first public school in that area. It was named Pleasant Hill School. They were all church going people. The Grables helped to start the Bethesda Methodist Church. The Cranfills started the Disciples of Christ Church. Bethesda Methodist has been rebuilt recently (2004) on the same property. My family and I have attended several reunions of the three original families in the Bethesda community and church. The three families were Simmons, Smith and Grable. My great grandmother Grable was a Simmons. The reunion is held on the third Saturday of June each year from 11 a.m. to 3 p.m. The fellowship and food are wonderful. The Bethesda Cemetery is just across the road from the church. Many members of our Grable family are buried there. Another cemetery, named Authon cemetery is about 2 miles north and east of Bethesda. Many Cranfills and Grables are buried there. This cemetery bears a historical marker. My Uncle Paul Grable, Dad's youngest brother, was there for that dedication as were my husband and I. That was in the early 1970's.

Louise Grable Boyd holding 1st born Bobby, John F. Grable, and his mother, Jane Cranfill Grable at the Cranfill reunion in Buffalo Gap 1938

My mother's sister, Elizabeth and her husband, Eli Vance moved to Throckmorton and persuaded Mom & Dad to sell out and go WEST. It seems most people thought if you moved west, you would become rich. Not so in our case! My parent's farm was located 7 miles northeast of Throckmorton on Highway 79; about 6 miles west of Elbert and 23 miles northwest of Olney, Texas. At the time they purchased the farm, there were no paved roads. The farm was about 1 1/2 miles south of the "highway". Anytime we tried to leave the farm after a heavy rain we would get stuck in the draw (low place in the road) between our house and the Keeter family place. Dad used to carry pieces of cardboard, etc. to put behind the wheels to get traction when the car got stuck. In 1976, I sold ½ of my half of the farm to my Boyd nephews. We needed the money to add

Wilson Lee Brakle
Sept 25 – 1827
Dec 6th – 1883 ~ 56¾
Buried north of road from
Adell to Bethesda

Wiley Harris Road from Crosel
town of W.L. Brakle which was
to say Home Built by W.L. Brakle
He left Brakle road buried
He went Cemetery He
wanted first one
but first

Mary Ann Brakle
June 18 – 1830 ~ 78 yrs
June 10 – 1908
Buried at Bethesda Yes
West of Weatherford Tx

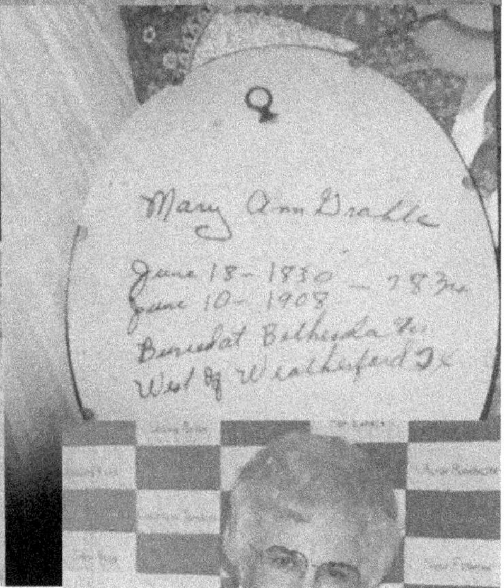

a room onto our home and to update the master bath. (I sold the rest of my share of the family farm in October of 1996 to Mike Lukert of Olney. I retained my 1/16 of the mineral rights on the 160 acres on the west side of the road that divided the farm. At times I am sorry I sold it, but neither my husband, Joe, nor I are farmers and it was difficult to find reliable people to lease it. Had I kept it, it would be worth a lot more money now. Isn't that always the way!

Before I was born, my mother and her niece, Fannie Vance, went to West Texas Normal College in Canyon, Texas during the summer. My Aunt Betty Vance went along to take care of my sister, Louise, while Mother attended classes. Mother also attended North Texas Normal College (now known as North Texas State University) until she could obtain a teaching certificate. She taught at Carson school which was about three or four miles southwest of the farm. She was a born teacher— she really loved teaching and her students loved her. Mother taught until the State of Texas required a full four-year degree for teachers.

7-18-94

Dear Billie John,

Glad to hear from you and wish you success in writing your "Book"

The school that your mother taught was the Carson School. I started to school in September at the age of 5 yrs - in 1917 and we moved into Throckmorton in 1922.

I do not know how much longer the carson School continued.

She was dear to me and she spent several nights in our home when it rained and she could not get home. Just dirt roads at that time. It was a one room school with grades one through six. Sincerely Elsie

Mrs. Elsie Davis, Former student

Life on the farm was not what you would call easy. Our country bathroom was a "wooden outhouse" with 2 holes over a dugout. It was located about 100 yards north of the house. Our toilet tissue was a page out of the Sears & Roebuck or the Montgomery Ward catalog. Our bathtub was a No. 2 galvanized washtub moved into the middle of the kitchen on Saturday night and filled with warm water that had been heated in pans on the cook stove which was fueled with kerosene. Our "central heat" was a wood-burning stove in the front (south) bedroom. The living room was closed off all winter because it was on the north side and there was no way to heat it. There was no such thing as insulation in little farm houses in those days. Springtime was looked forward to with much anticipation because we could take the wood stove down thus making more room in the bedroom. Taking down the stovepipe was fun. The soot and ashes flew everywhere and had to be cleaned up. With warmer weather, the living room could now be opened. When my brother was home from college and working on the farm in the summer, he loved to call me into the dark living room and scare me. I was only five but, of course I loved it because I knew it was my brother.

When the weather made the roads impassable, Dad would get on his horse and ride into the pasture to hunt a rabbit. Mom would make a rabbit stew with dumplings which was delicious (this was before health laws). In icy, snowy weather, Dad would have to ride his horse to the dirt highway (no pavement) to get our mail. All the neighbors had a mailbox located next to the main road to make it easier for the mailman. If the weather stayed bad for long periods of time, which it did in those days, Dad would have to ride his horse the 7 miles into Throckmorton for supplies. Mother turned out great meals from that little country kitchen. When Dad was working in the fields, she prepared big, hearty breakfasts. Sometimes she prepared fried chicken, gravy and biscuits and on other occasions she cooked homemade sausage, gravy and biscuits. The syrup was almost always homemade by boiling sugar and water until it thickened. During harvesting season we might have 15 extra farmhands working the cutting and binding equipment. She had to prepare lunch and dinner for them. I can remember the men taking a siesta on our front porch and under the trees before going back to the hard work in the hot fields. The binder produced oblong bales of hay that were automatically formed and held together with baling wire. The oats and barley were stored in the granary near the barn. An interesting antidote is that our son, Michael, was able to remove metal signs that my father gathered along the highway to repair holes that mice made in the granary. Michael straightened them out, put a wooden backing on them and has them hanging in his den. One of them advertised Clabber Girl baking powder.

Mother and Dad always had a big garden on the south side of the house. Much canning and preserving of vegetables and fruit was done in the summer. My grandmother, Mary Elizabeth "Mammy" Vick, lived with us several months of each year and helped with the cooking and canning. The canned food was stored in an underground cellar in the back yard. On a warm summer day when I was about 4 or 5 my mother took some jars of food she had just canned into the cellar to put on the shelves. When she was ready to come out, a rattlesnake was coiled on one of the steps near the bottom. I was playing near the entrance so she yelled for me to run to the field in front of the house and get Daddy to come kill the snake. He saw me running toward the field so he stopped his team of horses and came running to meet me. When I told him the problem, he ran on to the house and got a hoe and killed the snake. I have a very vivid memory of that day plus I still have a great fear of any kind of snake.

In order to clean our clothes and linens, Dad would build a fire under the big black, iron "wash pot" to heat the water each Monday morning. Mother had to scrub the clothes on a metal rub board and then rinse them in a #2 galvanized washtub and wring out the water by hand. They were then hung on the clothesline to dry. This was very trying during cold weather. Mrs. Keeter, our closest neighbor, got a Maytag washing machine that was gasoline powered. We could hear the putt-putt of the engine clearly. Mother looked forward to the day she could have such a machine. She never got a gasoline-powered machine, but did get an electric-powered machine in 1933 after we moved to town. In order to provide me with art lessons mother washed and ironed clothes for the Presbyterian minister, Rev. Dooley and his family. Mrs. Dooley was a wonderful artist and teacher. I kept in touch with her until the mid 1960's. I took piano lessons from Mrs. Putnam for four years, but didn't do too well as I did not practice enough. Dad paid for the piano lessons with milk. Our milk cow was named Jersey Bell and she was a beauty.

In the springtime on the farm, mother and I would put on the headphones of our crystal radio set and listen to Jimmy Jeffries "Early Birds" program from Dallas (820 on the AM dial) before getting out of bed. The program was very entertaining and originated in the Baker Hotel. Unfortunately, the Baker Hotel was demolished in the late 1970's. It had been a beautiful building, but had served it's time.

Our closest neighbors were the Haile family on the west, the Hardy and Chandler families on the south and east, the Keeter family on the north and further north across the highway and behind the school I attended for kindergarten was the Garvin family. I loved to visit the Garvins on Sunday afternoons. They had 4 daughters older than I and they were very nice to me. Mrs. Garvin was like a grandmother -- she always served refreshments. She even let me play her pump organ. (I couldn't really play—just made noise.)

In 1928 the railroad was constructed from Graham to Throckmorton. This was cause for great celebration which was held on the main street of town on May 28, 1928. Indians came from Oklahoma in full regalia with bows and arrows. Buffalo had been imported from the northwest plains for a buffalo shoot. I was looking forward to seeing the Indians ride their horses and kill the buffalo, but before the shoot was to take place, I got a cinder in my eye. I also needed to go to the bathroom. I was four and a half at the time. Mother took me to Aunt Alpha Brown's home where my grandmother Vick was staying. While I was

indisposed, my mother left to go back to the activities. I cried and howled the rest of the afternoon. I'm surprised my grandmother Vick did not take "a switch" to me. The county gave the Buffalo meat to families that could use it. The panoramic photograph (previous page) was given to me by my sister's two sons and their wives. Fifteen thousand people descended on Throckmorton to see the train come in. (The normal population was about one thousand). Believe it or not, my handsome father is near the left side of this photograph wearing his 10-gallon hat and his dress suit. I am so delighted to have this.

Our farmhouse was very small. It probably had no more than 900 square feet. It had a kitchen and eating area along the back (west side) of the house. The living room and bedroom were across the front of the house with a door between the rooms and a door in each room that opened onto the front porch. It had a roofed porch across the front of the house and an open porch on the back. Many times I would lie on the back porch looking up at the sky trying to figure out which cloud looked like a dog, etc. A window was located in the north end of the kitchen. The window was free of the sun's rays most of the day so dad placed a screened box in the window during the summer. The bottom of the box consisted of a metal pan about four inches deep. About 3 inches of water would be placed in the metal floor making the box act as a refrigerator of sorts. A wet cloth covered the screening thus making it cool when the wind blew across it. Mother would then store left-over food plus milk and butter in the box. We had a wooden ice box in which to store food also. The ice storage compartment was lined with zinc so the block (50 lb.) of ice wouldn't melt so fast. The other compartment was for food storage. In the summer little black sugar ants came out so my parents had to set the dining table legs in low tin cans filled with water to keep the ants off the table. We had a telephone, but there were about 8 homes on the party line. For those of you who never experienced a party line—it simply means all the people on the line can listen in on each other's conversations if they so desire. Hopefully their conscience didn't let them do this often. Calls were distinguished by so many short rings and so many long rings for each party. When we heard "one long and one short" ring, we knew it was our call. We had no electricity just a kerosene lamp.

Of course there was no running water. We had a stone and concrete lined cistern. Dad had a Model "T" truck with a water tank on it. He used it to haul water from town to fill the cistern with drinking and cooking water. A large metal tank about 12 feet high was located at the northwest corner of the house to catch rainwater from the roof. This tank helped shade the cooler in the kitchen window. The water caught in this tank was used to wash clothes and put water out for the chickens and turkeys to drink.

Mrs. Hardy was the teacher at Oak Grove School about two miles north of our house. The school had 7 grades plus kindergarten in that one room. I was a kindergartener. In order to get to the school, a creek had to be crossed. My teacher and I rode her horse to school when the creek was impassable by car and when the weather was snowy and/or icy. The rest of the time I rode with her in her little ford coupe. My mother prepared a lunch for me to take to school each day. I carried the lunch in a small round KARO SYRUP bucket that had a "bail" for a handle. My dessert was a cold biscuit spread with butter that had sugar sprinkled on it. My favorite sandwich was a cold biscuit with a sausage patty on it. Fresh fruit was a seasonal treat because little fruit was shipped in those days--at least not to Throckmorton. I only went to the Oak Grove School for my kindergarten year because Mother and Dad bought a lot in town and built a duplex. Building a new house in the depression required a lot of nerve. My parents had a very difficult time paying for the farm and the house during those depression years. They were very frugal people thus they accomplished their goal.

When I was born my brother was attending Hardin Simmons College in Abilene and my sister was attending Throckmorton High School. Due to the bad roads in winter, my sister took room and board with the A. A. Boyd family. They lived just about a block from the school so she could walk to school. Thomas, their son, was attending Hardin Simmons University in Abilene. When Thomas and my sister started dating, I always wanted to tag along. They were very sweet to let me do this--especially Sunday afternoons when they went for a ride. They went in a coupe and I usually rode up behind the seat. I can remember when Thomas kissed my sister I would get so upset I would

want to hit him. They thought that was funny but I thought he was mistreating my sister.

Shortly after moving to Throckmorton in 1919, my parents were "in the money" for a while. They had a good production year from the farm and had sold the business in Whitt, Texas. They purchased a new 4-door Model "A" Ford and took a trip to San Antonio to visit Dad's sister Mary Grable Fitts and her family. The inflation was helping everyone. They failed to realize the BIG DEPRESSION starting in 1929 would soon leave them short of income. My brother attended college at Canyon Normal College, Canyon, Texas; Tarleton College, Stephenville, Texas; and finally graduated from Hardin Simmons, a Baptist College in Abilene, Texas. My sister attended Texas Wesleyan College in Fort Worth following high school graduation. In the fall semester she transferred to Hardin Simmons where she was initiated into the (then famous) Cowgirl marching group and service organization. I have always said mother and dad spent all their money on brother and sister going to expensive schools was why I had to go to North Texas State Teachers college. Louise had completed two years of college when she was elected by the Carson school board to teach beginning the fall 1927. This country school was located about two miles southwest of our farm. The following year she taught at Padgett, a little town 1½ miles northeast of Elbert. She took room and board with a family there. On March 8, 1930 she married Thomas E. Boyd in our family living room in Throckmorton. The Presbyterian minister who lived in the Presbytery just east of mother & dad officiated. I remember going to Breckenridge to shop for her trousseau and wedding dress. Her dress was brown crepe decorated with brown satin. It was the "flapper" style of the day; draped short skirt, long sleeves, and high neckline. I thought she was a beautiful bride.

Louise 1926

My brother graduated from Hardin Simmons with a degree in education and math in May of 1929. On June 5, 1929 he married his college sweetheart, Beulah Low Lee who had graduated from McMurray College in Abilene. They had a large formal wedding at the First Methodist Church in Throckmorton. (See Article in Appendix) I was a flower girl as was my good friend, Precious Parrott. We wore matching dresses of orchid and pink organdy. The skirt was long and consisted of many layers of ruffles. We thought we were pretty special five year olds, but that organdy sure did scratch. Following the reception, the couple left for Galveston on their honeymoon.

I need to insert some remembrances about the Lee family here. Father Lee was considered wealthy by most standards in those days. He owned a lot of land in New Mexico and kept it stocked with Hereford cattle as well as his ranch in Throckmorton. Augie Mae was their oldest daughter and she taught at Texas Wesleyan College in Ft. Worth. (Her husband died at a young age of a heart attack.) She had a daughter, Jane, who was my age. When they came to Throckmorton to visit, I was invited to play with Jane. The Lee home was a two story home and very pretty. Since I had never lived in a two story home, it was fun to climb up and down the stairs. Jane and I were allowed to go to the garage apartment to play sometimes too because we could play dress-up in discarded clothing that was up there. Our family was invited to the Lee home for lunch at Thanksgiving several times. Father Lee always sat at the head of the table dressed in suit, white shirt and tie. He would stand to carve the turkey, place pieces on each plate and pass the plates until everyone was served. This made quite an impression on this little country girl. One year at Christmas, Mother Lee gave me a small metal jewelry box that was embossed on top with a forest scene. I used it to keep my hairpins in for many years. Not long ago my daughter said she wanted it because of the stories I used to tell her about visiting in the Lee home. So, Carol Ann is now the owner of the metal box. The top hinge broke so Joe had to repair it with small hinges held in place with screws and nuts.

The fall following their wedding, Low and John A. both taught school in Woodson, Texas. It was a real treat for me to spend a weekend with them which I did often. I was also invited to spend a week or two with them in the summer which I really enjoyed. They both spoiled me which I loved. Low would heat her curling iron in a kerosene lamp and put curls in my very straight hair. I loved that because I always wanted long curls like most of my friends. My hair was so thick and straight that Mother kept it cut in a Buster Brown style most of the time. Those of you too young to remember, there used to be a brand of socks for children named Buster Brown. A small picture of "Buster Brown" was on the label attached to each pair of socks and he had very short hair over his ears, bangs and shingled up the back as a boy's haircut would have been, thus the Buster Brown haircut. The summer of 1930, Brother and Low went to the World's Fair in Chicago and reportedly had a wonderful time. That fall brother was the football coach in Woodson. Back then, the community would grade off a plot of ground in a pasture for the field. The players wore caps similar to aviator caps. I don't know how they stood to play on hard ground with no pads like they have today.

1. Willie Laura Vick, b. 6 Oct. 1886
2. Mary Jemima Vick, b. 11 Oct 1878
3. Daniel Aswell Vick, b. 24 April 1882
4. Nancy Elizabeth Vick, b. 13 Sept. 1871
5. Frances Vick, b. 25 July 1875
6. Loyd Brown, b. 21 Nov. 1894
7. Lewis Brown, b. 18 August 1870
8. Nathan Monroe Vick, b. 15 Dec. 1850
9. Mary Elizabeth Lopp Vick, b. 22 Sept. 1854

My Vick grandparents (Mary Elizabeth and Nathan Monroe) are buried in the Whitt, Texas cemetery just inside the fence to the right of the entrance gate. "Pappy" died of Bright's disease according to the death certificate. Mammy always said he died of influenza. (Photos of their headstones are in the Appendix along with death certificates.) After Pappy's death, my grandmother, Mary Elizabeth (Lopp) Vick, lived with each of her four daughters three months of the year. Mammy's father, William M. Lopp is buried in a CAIRN in the Gilead cemetery in Keller, Texas. (A cairn is a wall made of stone that goes around a grave but there is no longer identification at the cairns so we can't identify his.) I am not sure where her Mother is buried. She may have died when they went to California during the "gold rush".

Mary Elizabeth?
Nathan Monroe Vick's daughters

Frances Stuart
Vick Brown
Mama E
Vick Shasley

Nancy Elizabeth
Vick Vance

Daniel Crucil Simpson
Vick King

Tillie Laura
Vick Grable

The grandchildren all called my grandmother Mammy. When she was with our family, she had a lot of influence on me. She taught me to dress and comb my hair first thing each morning because as she put it "you never knew who might come calling". I was to keep my shoes polished. I was never to work on Sunday. She kept her sewing or crocheting in a little fold-up type carrier. About 3 p.m. on Saturday, this box was closed and not opened again until Monday morning. She taught me how to make and apply the fringe to her hand-crocheted bedspreads and even paid me a quarter to help do it. Mammy helped mother with the cooking. She made the most fabulous buttermilk pie I ever ate. Mammy was also a great quilt-maker. Her favorite design was the double wedding-ring pattern. After completing the quilt top, the cotton bats had to be made by "carding" cotton. My Aunt Alpha Brown kept a quilting frame in her living room most all winter. Several women would get together and quilt most of the day stopping just long enough to eat lunch. By spring each woman had one or two new quilts for her family to use for warmth the next winter. I still have a quilt Mammy made for me—the pattern is Dutch Boy and Girl. After completing a quilt top, cotton "bats" had to be made by hand and applied to the lining of the quilt. They took raw cotton and "carded it to make the bats. They used wooden carding tools to which they applied the cotton onto thousands of small teeth. (You can look up the definition)

Mammy was staying with my Aunt Fannie Brown in Perrin, Texas when she wrote me a letter saying she was not feeling well. She said she felt like a piece of ice that was slowly melting. She was 84 years old and her body was wearing out. Just a few days after I received that letter, we got word that she had died. I was 13 at the time and felt like I had lost my best friend.

When I was ten or twelve years of age my brother, John Aaron Grable purchased a Chevrolet dealership in Merkel, Texas (about 15 miles west of Abilene). He was always trading for things. One weekend he brought a black and white Shetland pony, named Queenie, to Throckmorton for my sister's son, Bobby, and me to ride and care for. Queenie was black and white; so pretty and so gentle. We had many joyful hours riding Queenie until brother felt it was time to sell her. Later, brother bought a used bicycle, painted it red, put new tires on it and brought it to me. I had many falls before I learned to ride on that rocky hillside by our house. I enjoyed visiting my brother and his wife; especially after their sons John Robert (born in 1937) and Jerry Lee (born in 1939) were born. It was fun babysitting them from time to time. Having an older brother and sister that loved me was wonderful.

During WWII, it became impossible to obtain new cars to sell so brother sold his dealership and he, Beulah Low and the boys moved to Throckmorton. Low taught the third grade in Throckmorton elementary school. My parents and Low's mother put up money to help brother buy a small ranch east of Throckmorton. I was told the money my parents put up was to be part of his inheritance. He stocked his land with cattle and did a lot of trading of cattle. He was also a salesman for Farmers Insurance of some kind. I can't remember which company.

My sister was always doing things to enhance our learning as well as provide fun times for us. She bought a small tent for her son, Bobby and me. She would let us fry potatoes over coals in front of the tent. We thought we were big campers. On July fourth, sister would fry chicken, make a freezer of ice cream and we (my parents and Sister's family) would go to the creek not too far from their farm and fish before having lunch. By the time we got home in the afternoon, we usually had a dozen or more "chigger" bites plus some fish. The fun we had made it worthwhile.

My mother bought a portable Singer sewing machine for me when I was in the ninth grade. She did this so I could make my own clothes. When I was a junior in Throckmorton High School, I won a trip to Dallas as a contestant at the Future Homemakers of America (FHA) convention. I modeled the dress I had made in class as part of the competition. My dress was constructed of black (with small white dots) chiffon-like fabric. The yoke was tucked and the skirt was flared. I thought it was beautiful. Mother purchased a lovely picture-brimmed hat for me to wear in the modeling. I won honorable mention. The other category I entered was "Furnishing a specified living space." I won a third place ribbon in that category making my teacher and me very happy. We were in Dallas three wonderful days and stayed at the Baker Hotel. Before leaving for Dallas my father gave me a watch with two little diamond chips in the case. Father kept a milk cow in town on a small plot of land owned by my Aunt Alpha & Uncle Loyd Brown. Dad had 3 or 4 milk customers. One of the customers was Mr. Cowan, the local jeweler. That was how dad paid for the watch. I was very proud of this, my first watch, and wore it many years. I still have it although it no longer works.

The "great depression" hit about the time our house in town was completed. My father suffered a devastating heart attack in 1933 or 1934 following extraction of all his teeth by a dentist in Mineral Wells. My father was very sick for two or three years and never fully recovered. He always suffered from angina. He could never do hard physical work following his heart attack. Thus, it was primarily up to mother to make the living. To do so, she always kept roomers, boarders, and rented out one side of the duplex. In addition to roomers and boarders, she bought and sold produce (butter, eggs, and chickens). She had a regular route of farmers that sold to her twice a week. After she picked up the eggs, we would "candle" the eggs to make sure they were good. If you are not familiar with the candling process; it was done by holding the egg before a small light encased in a box to make sure there were no cloudy spots in the egg. In the event there were spots, this meant the egg was bad. This was done in our garage where it was somewhat dark. Mother had regular customers that purchased the produce from her in Wichita Falls and Breckenridge Texas. They operated grocery stores and restaurants. This was before they had health laws. The profits she derived from this endeavor helped put me through high school and college. In the fall she bought turkeys all over the county and arranged for a produce company from Fort Worth to purchase the turkeys from her. They sent trucks to Throckmorton to pick them up. They came for the turkeys at night because turkeys were more docile and easier to handle at night.

When we moved to town from the farm the school officials let me skip first grade. I guess Mrs. Hardy must have done a good job teaching me in kindergarten. Mrs. Fred Harrell (our Doctor's wife) was my second grade teacher. She was a very good teacher and also very kind and loving. My third grade teacher was Miss Dora Holt whom I loved very much. I got letters and Christmas cards from her until her death in about 1983. She, too, was a very special person. My fourth grade teacher was

1932

Miss Elizabeth Donnell (a relative of the Donnells of Throckmorton and Eliasville). I liked her but she was not as loving as the previous teachers. My fifth grade teacher was Miss Lera D. Irick. She was a tall, large lady and I was scared to death of her. As strange as it seems, when Joe and I moved to Dallas in 1952 I started substitute teaching

BILLIE JOHN GRABLE - ABT 1934

and who should I run into at one of the schools where I did a lot of substituting but Miss Irick. She was very friendly and happy to see me. She passed away in the early 1980's. Mr. Hizer was my 6th grade social studies teacher as well as elementary principal. Mrs. Peavy was my math teacher. She ran a very strict class. If a boy misbehaved, he got his hand spanked with a ruler. If a girl misbehaved, her face was dusted with an eraser. Thank goodness I

22

never misbehaved in her class. This was because I loved her. My high school teachers were exceptional for a small town. I especially enjoyed my Home Economics, Science, English and Band teachers. The reason I say I had some good teachers is because when I went to college, I was put in several advanced classes. The high school principal, Alfred S. Jackson and his wife lived in the west side of our duplex. He was my high school chemistry teacher and a very good one. Mr. Jackson attended our 1984 homecoming. He looked just about like he did when I was in high school.

Neighbors always came on hog-killing day to help Dad with the butchering, rendering of lard, cooking "chittlins" and rolling the hams in brown sugar and salt for curing. The sugar and salt preserved the meat and kept it from spoiling IF the weather stayed cool. The meat was stored in the smokehouse. Following the hog killing, my mother made lye soap using scraps of fat from the hog. I don't have the recipe, but she made it in her big "black iron wash pot." After cooking, the content was allowed to cool down and set up for several days. Once it had hardened, Mom and Dad would cut the soap into squares. This soap was used for washing our clothes. The lye supposedly killed all germs. My daughter has this wash pot in her backyard and uses it as a planter for flowers.

June, Glow, Minta Sue, ?, Adrienne, Billie John, Sallie Lou, ? Bobbie Nell, Francie ?

Fourth Grade Class
1933-34

Teacher- Miss Donnell in back

23

BILLIE GRABLE WITH FRIENDS HOME FROM SCHOOL IN 1944

While in grade school, some of my friends and I played "school" almost every afternoon. I always wanted to be "the teacher." Sallie Lou Tharp, Adrienne Smith, Glow Rhoades, Ray Laverne Fry, Mary Ethel Tenney and Minta Sue Thompson were some of my favorite friends. Glow passed away in the late 1970s, but I still keep in touch with the others. (Photo is of some of this group reunited for an afternoon when home from college.) In Junior High we formed the "Gigglers Club". We could giggle about anything and usually did. In high school Sallie Lou, Adrienne and I were in the band along with Janice Pogue, Adrienne's cousin. During my first year in the band I played a trumpet. Sallie Lou's home had an upstairs balcony that faced the school grounds. We used to sit on the balcony after school to practice on our instruments. I bet the neighbors enjoyed that! My second year in band I played a Tenor Saxophone. I loved it but had to face up to the fact that I was not a musician; therefore, I joined the Pep Squad for my senior year. I think this is the reason for my voice tremor -- I simply yelled too much and too loud for our football team during their games.

My parents and I attended the First Methodist Church. My father was on the Board of Stewards when the present church was built in 1929. I felt called to join the church at the age of nine. When I was 10, I attended summer church camp near Abilene for a week. It was during this week that I truly came to feel God's presence in my life. I was very active in Sunday

First Methodist Church
Throckmorton

school, the choir, and Epworth League; later renamed M.Y.F. (Methodist Youth Fellowship). Mr. Pat Cochran was our sponsor. Pat was a cashier at the First National Bank in Throckmorton. He was about 25 at the time. At this writing (2008), he is living in Houston.

My mother, my sister, Aunt Alpha, Uncle Loyd, John Lee and Kathryn and I decided to take a little trip to Carlsbad Caverns in 1937. We drove to Wink, Texas to visit cousins Frank Heasley, his wife and children. They decided to come along on the trip. Their daughter, Rouye, Kathryn and I had a lot of fun on the trip. While we were in Wink, we also visited Violet Blackburn and her family. Frank & Violet were brother and sister and children of my Aunt Mima. Their baby brother, Dell, lived in Houston. Cousin Kittie Vance and her son, Kenneth, went on this trip with us. They rode in Uncle Loyd's pickup with him and his family. Kenneth rolled out of the pickup onto the highway somewhere between Wink and El Paso. We all just knew he was dead, but he just had a few scrapes. The trip was wonderful. The Caverns were beautiful. When the lights were turned out as we sat in the Palace Room, a singing group sang "Rock of Ages". It was so dark you couldn't see your hand in front of your face.

Small west Texas towns were short on entertainment-- especially Throckmorton. Part of the fun things we experienced included traveling medicine shows, tent shows, a small circus now and then and a traveling skating rink. When the medicine show came to town, a truck-drawn trailer would open up as their stage and a drama of some kind would be presented. Benches were set up for the audience to sit on. At intermission, circus staff members would walk through the audience selling their wares. The Haverstock Tent Show Organization came to town at least once a year—they presented some of the best dramas this side of New York. The children enjoyed intermission because a red-haired clown called Toby entertained them. These dramatic presentations were for us what Broadway shows were for New Yorkers. Mr. Haverstock was a talented person - he was an actor and musician. His show was on the tent circuit from 1911 to 1954 (see my copy of the book-The History of the Haverstock Tent Show by Robert Lee Wyatt III).

A traveling skating-rink came to town in the spring and it would stay from 2 to 4 weeks. Skating to our favorite tunes with our favorite partners was fun. Some of the young people skated in trios and "dipped in and out" around the floor keeping time to the beautiful music. The good skaters were beautiful to watch. I was never good at sports. I was a substitute on the volleyball team my junior and senior years of high school. My main interests were sewing and crafts hence my college major was Home Economics. I will elaborate more about these interests later.

My friend Ray Laverne Fry and her parents invited me to go with them on their summer vacation in 1939. We drove to Colorado Springs the first day. The next day we went up Pike's Peak. That was quite a thrill. I was able to send my parents a telegram from there for twenty five cents. We continued on to Yellowstone Park. We saw several bears and other animals not seen in Texas. Old Faithful was certainly unique and most beautiful. We stayed in a lovely cabin. This was quite a trip for a little country girl.

When I was a high school junior, my classmates selected me "favorite girl" and "most beautiful". They didn't have many to choose from. HA! I was selected as the homecoming football queen when I was a senior student. The announcement was made at "half-time" of the homecoming football game. The band had constructed a large jug made of a wooden frame covered with brown paper. When the band played "Little Brown Jug", the jug with me inside was carried onto the football field. As the announcement of the winner was made, I tore open the paper and jumped out. This was quite a thrill for a small town girl to be so honored in front of the townspeople. My crown was made of pliable cardboard covered with tinfoil wrappers from Wrigley's chewing gum. Back then we couldn't afford tiaras.

My graduation from high school was an exciting time. I received many nice useful gifts. We had a junior-senior banquet a few weeks before school was out. The girls wore formals and the boys wore "Sunday" suits. We had music and a speaker for entertainment. Of course the food was delicious. The decorations committee, of which I was a member, had fun decorating the auditorium which was on the third floor of the school building. Since that time it has been replaced with a newer, more modern one-story building. In those days we were not allowed to dance in Throckmorton because "we would go to hell" if we danced.

I need to digress here and tell you about my cousins Kathryn and John Lee Brown. When our family moved to town from the farm, their home was just about a half a block east of my home. We played together all summer either at their home or mine. We used a tin can at both ends of a long heavy twine string that reached from their house to mine as our telephone. We just knew we could hear each other. We would use any mud puddle to fish for crayfish. If we caught enough, we would clean and fry the tails. They tasted like shrimp. All in all it was nice to have cousins close enough to share life with. Kathryn and I used to draw and paint pictures together. We went to movies occasionally (cost in those days was 10 cents) played croquet, baseball, dominoes, etc. Uncle Loyd had built a croquet court just south of their house. It was used by many friends. To earn the money to go to the movies, we would gather and sell scrap iron. We never questioned why anyone would want to buy it, but later found that it was being sold to Japan. I'm sure they used it to make things to be used against us in WWII.

A few weeks after graduation, my cousin John Lee and four of our friends; Ruth Horton, Bobbie Nell Burkhalter, Treva Mae McNutt and her nephew Louie Glenn decided to drive 30 miles north to Seymour to visit two girls the boys had been dating. I was at Aunt Alpha and Uncle Lloyd Brown's home when the kids left. They invited me to go with them but I declined as I had a date. About an hour later "THE CALL" came from Seymour that the car they were in had been hit by a train. The car had been pushed several hundred feet along the track - it was a mass of twisted metal. Everyone was killed instantly except John Lee. He had massive head injuries and was in a coma for several days. The doctors had to put a steel plate in the upper left side of his head. He remained in the hospital several weeks. He eventually recovered and was in the army for nine months. He was given an honorable discharge because of his severe headaches. He then went to school at North Texas State where he met and married the campus beauty, Martha Murray. They had three sons: John, Jeff and Jack. John Lee departed this earth at age 65 on July 19, 1989 in Galveston. He had suffered from emphysema for several years. The death of these four young people was one of the saddest occasions that ever occurred in Throckmorton County prior to World War II. I have tears in my eyes while writing about this because we were all such good friends and they were very bright young people with promising futures. Their funerals were held in the High School Gymnasium so there would be room for all the people who wanted to attend.

In September of 1941 I enrolled at North Texas State Teachers College in Denton. My major was Home Economics and my minor was Business Education. My cousin, Kathryn Brown, and I were roommates in Culbertson Hall where she was the "housemother". The College had purchased 6 or 8 two-story houses and moved them onto a block of Avenue A just south of the campus. There was a central hall in the inside of the block that housed the cafeteria. We also had our own laundry where we washed things by hand. The purpose of these houses was to provide low-cost housing for students who could not afford to live in the dormitories. During my freshman year I had a part-time job working evenings in the office of Oak Street Hall (a dorm for girls). My primary duty was to operate the switchboard.

Upon returning from church on Sunday, Dec.7th, 1941, we learned via radio that Pearl Harbor, Hawaii had been bombed by the Japanese. Most of our navy vessels had been sunk. Consequently, most all of the boys on campus either volunteered or were drafted into military service immediately. The young men left on campus were designated as 4-F meaning they had some type of health problem. This was definitely a sad, distressful time.

During my junior and senior years I lived in a private three-story home along with several other students. The home was owned by a Mrs. Hodge and was designated "The Hodge House". We all loved her very much. The house was located on west Hickory Street directly across from the School Administration Building. During the summer school session, between my junior and senior year, my roommate was Bonnie Mask (later Russell was added as her married name). Bonnie is still living and in a retirement home here in Dallas. We met for lunch occasionally. We had a fun time that summer. We took sunbaths on the third floor porch in our bathing suits - very risqué! Then one night we decided to climb down the fire escape to see if we could elude Mr. Starr, the campus night watchman. About an hour later we climbed back up having successfully eluded him. The last summer I attended college, I finally got to live in Marquis Hall. It was the prettiest girl's dorm on campus. I worked the switchboard in the office there too.

On Sunday, July 4, 1943 the young ladies still on campus for summer school experienced an exciting event. About noon the train arrived with 250 young soldiers to attend NTSU for training as Engineers. Their program was called "The Army Specialized Training Program" (A.S.T.P. Unit 3890). At that time I was an employee at Voertman's Fountain and Book/Gift Store. In the late afternoon and evening, the soldiers were free to move around campus as they saw fit. One evening when I was working behind the fountain, this tall, good looking soldier came in and sat in a booth. I walked back to take his order. I said, "Hi soldier" why are you looking so sad? He said he had just received a letter from his girlfriend and she was planning to join the Catholic Convent. Needless to say, I tried to remove his sadness. Two years later we became husband and wife. We have been married 63 years as of May 12, 2008.

We had fun dating for almost 8 weeks before the A.S.T.P. program was disbanded and Joe was transferred to Camp Howze on the outskirts of Gainesville, TX. Twice a month N.T.S.T.C. would send 2 busloads of girls to Camp Howze to dance with the soldiers. Joe did not dance at that time, so we sat and talked. Other weekends, when not on maneuvers in the field, Joe would come to Denton. That was how it went until July of 1944 when Joe was once again sent to Camp Robinson in Arkansas for six months.

I graduated from North Texas in August, 1944 and moved to Austin where I shared an apartment with cousin Kathryn and Kathryn Quackenbush. I worked as secretary to three lawyers until January when I moved back to Throckmorton to teach business courses in the high school. The business teacher had resigned. Joe had once again been transferred; this time to Fort Sill, Oklahoma. By moving home, I could go to Wichita Falls, Texas where Joe would meet me on weekends. By the end of March we decided we really were in love and made the decision to get married on May 12th, 1945.

Engagement Photo
April 1945

On May 12th, my sister, my cousin Kathryn, my nephew Bobby, and I were to pick Joe up in Fort Sill and drive back to Wichita Falls for our wedding at 7p.m. (We had to stop in Wichita Falls to buy my wedding dress, shoes, etc.) When we arrived in Fort Sill, the officer of the day told us Joe had taken the bus into town to buy my wedding ring. We took off for Lawton to find the jewelers and Joe to no avail. We went back to camp and were told Joe had taken the bus back to town to look for us. We were too frantic to stop and stay put; therefore we didn't get together until almost 6 p.m. We had to call my cousin, Fannye Vance who had arranged for us to be married in the First Methodist Church, and tell her we were going to be about 3 hours late. By the time we got to W.F., showered, dressed, and got to the church it was 11:30 p.m. The organist had given up and gone home. We were married by Joe Z.

Tower, head pastor of the church and father of former Texas Senator John Tower. Following the ceremony, our family peppered us with rice and we left for our room at the Kemp Hotel. Kathryn Brown and John Lee Brown were our attendants. About 20 family members were in attendance; Mother and Dad, Brother, Low and the boys (John R. & Jerry), Sister, Thomas and the boys (Bobby and Tommy), Aunt Alpha and Uncle Loyd, Cousin Fannye Vance (who lived and taught school in Wichita Falls) and her roommate, Hattie. It was too late to even have a reception.

Our Wedding Photo, May 12, 1945

Sunday morning, we dutifully rose and went to church. We went to a movie that afternoon, and spent another night at the Kemp Hotel. Joe had to leave at 5 a.m. to get back to Ft. Sill. I took the bus back to Throckmorton to finish out the last two weeks of the school year. We made a family photo the next weekend after Joe arrived from Ft. Sill. (see next page)

Mother had a friend, Kate Thomas, who knew a lady in Ft. Sill that was good enough to rent me a room until I could find a place for Joe & me to live. The lady was very good to me as Joe was in the field on maneuvers when I arrived. Each morning I would go to the U.S.O. (United Service Organization) and get a list of apartments for rent to

servicemen. I finally found a one-room apartment close to the bus line (we had no car) so we could get to and from the Base. This one room contained a double bed, a dresser, chest of drawers, a small old-time wooden ice box, a two burner gas stove w/oven, and an old fashioned safe. The safe had storage for dishes above the pull-out counter, a storage canister for flour with a sifter on the bottom, plus storage below the counter for pots & pans. This counter was the only workspace for preparing food. The bathroom was shared with the owner. After living there a while, we learned she was a "lady of the night." We lived there about three months. We were fortunate to find a new duplex and lived there about three months. At that time, Joe made Staff/Sgt. which allowed us to move on base and live in military housing for $30.00 a month. This duplex was huge compared to our other two domains. We had a bedroom, a living room, and a kitchen large enough for a table & two chairs. We purchased an unfinished table and two chairs in Lawton. I was so proud of them. Before Joe could put a finish on the wood, I baked a cake and put it on wax paper on my new table to cool. The heat from the cake melted the wax paper and I had a permanent circle on my table. The army had a resale shop for personnel who were shipping out to other posts or overseas. That was where we were able to purchase some furnishings. The army furnished beds for the apt.

until we could buy what we needed. We probably spent $100.00 to furnish the place.

While we lived in Lawton and Fort Sill, I worked as a secretary for the Officer of the Day at the Post Hospital. The army personnel I worked for were very nice to me. One day shortly after I started working at the Post Hospital, I heard an ambulance come roaring in. Sgt. Vandergriff said, "Here comes the meat wagon". He explained this was their slang for the men being brought in from the

Christmas 1945

field who had either been injured or killed while on exercises. We attended the First Methodist Church while living in Lawton. For entertainment, we played tennis, went to movies and even went to an equestrian place and rode horses once. During the summer of 1945, there was a truck drivers strike in Illinois. The army sent Joe's unit to give the non-striking drivers safe passage through Chicago. The boys were camped on the beach next to Lake Michigan on Lincoln Boulevard. Upon returning to Ft. Sill, after about three weeks, Joe's unit packed all of their belongings and equipment which was sent to Seattle. They were to ship out for overseas duty, but the tour of duty was canceled as the war was drawing to a close—THANK GOODNESS!!! Joe was sent to Camp Atterbury, Indiana to be discharged in February, 1946.

Joe registered at the University of Texas Engineering School in Austin the first of March 1946. The college had about 14,000 freshman GIs wanting to register. The university immediately went to the tri-mester program. BUT, freshmen could only register IF they had a place to live. I arrived in Austin while Joe was in Indianapolis being discharged. Each morning I went to the office of the Dean of Housing and got in line to get a list of available housing. Then I would go by taxi to the different addresses to see if the apartment was available. After a week of this, I located a small apt. in back of a lovely home in West Austin on Castle Hill Road. This small apt. was previously used as servant's quarters. The home was owned by The Nathan J. Hirsch family. They owned a chain of 3 or 4 drugstores in Austin at the time. We had two small rooms. At least we had an address so Joe could register at U.T. When Joe arrived in Austin in civilian clothes, I was shocked. I said to myself, "Is this the man I married?" Men do look different in civilian clothes. The apt. had a combination bedroom-eating area and a combination bath-kitchen. This was the only place we ever lived that I could sit on the "pot" and "stir the beans" at the same time. The bedroom had a ¾ bed, our tiny table & two chairs. I bought a cardboard closet for our hanging clothes and we kept our "undies" under the bed in our suitcases. Austin is very humid in the summer (and had no air conditioning at that time) so our suitcases mildewed. One night one of the bedposts went through the rotting flooring to the ground (about 4 inches). That was exciting. We used our same little table and chairs here that were purchased in Ft. Sill. It was in this small apt. where our daughter, Carol Ann, was conceived. When I told my mother I was pregnant, her observation was: "I knew when you told me about that small bed you had, you would get pregnant".

The Hirsch family left in June for a trip to California. Mrs. Hirsch told us to use their kitchen as if it were ours while they were gone. One night I turned on the gas oven—it had an automatic pilot light. I was cooking other food on the surface units and when I opened the oven to put the biscuits in, the pilot light was out and the gas that had accumulated in the oven caught fire from the surface units and there was quite an explosion in the kitchen. Joe came running from our apt. and found me on the floor in a daze. He saw my hands and arms were burned and I had no eyebrows and the front of my hair was singed off. He called for an ambulance and I was taken to the hospital for treatment. I had some second degree burns and spent 3 or 4 days in the hospital. When the Hirsch family returned, I was in their home in their bed nursing my burns. They were just happy I wasn't hurt any worse.

I got a job working as a secretary at the Electrical Engineering Research Lab. on campus shortly after arriving in Austin. I think I made $120.00 a month. The head secretary was Linnie Schieffer. She was like my second mother and became a life long friend. When I worked on campus, Joe & I walked to U.T. most of the time. Austin is up one hill and down and back up again. When I really started getting large with "little bit", Joe would push me up the hills. After a few months, we found a nice room w/bath just 3 or 4 blocks from the campus where we lived until the University moved in old army barracks and actually made a complex for veterans near Lake Austin called Brackenridge apartments. Quanset huts were moved in closer to the Lake for couples without children. Helen and James Tartt from Houston lived in one of those. Helen worked for EERL too. After Carol Ann was born, EERL hired Joe to work part-time. I went back to work for them when Carol Ann was three.

Before we moved into this two story barracks apt, Joe sanded and varnished all the floors. Uncle Loyd was a trucker so Mother got him to move our furniture to Austin which was a big help. We moved in about the middle of August. Joe's parents packed and shipped Mary Jane's baby bed to Austin. (Mike and Pam refinished the bed for Jacob to use too.) Mom Jurlina must have had fun shopping because she sent us a whole layette for her first grandchild. Everything was lovely and we sure made use of the many things she sent.

 Two weeks after we moved into Brackenridge Apts. Ed & Ren Veigel moved in with their baby daughter, Sandra. (She is 63 at this writing and we still call her "Baby Sandy". Then Nettie and Jimmy Horn moved in; next came Mary & Johnny Peacock. We were all about the same age, all interested in our men getting their degrees and all had children within a few months of each other. Johnny Byron Peacock was born in March, 1947; Baby Sandy was born August 12, 1946; and Gaylene Horn was born somewhere between Carol Ann & Johnny Byron.

On November 25th, 1946 about 3 p.m. Mary and Johnny Peacock took me to Brackenridge Hospital as I was in the "throes" of labor pains. (They had a car and we didn't) When we walked into the hospital, the nurse looked at me and at Mary and said, "Which one is about to deliver"? Mary wasn't due until March so we got a big laugh out of that. In those days, we had no classes or instructions to prepare us for the baby's delivery, nor could a loved one stay in the labor or delivery room like they do today. I was in a huge circular room which contained about 20 cubicles. Each cubicle had an expectant mother in it in varying stages of labor; most of whom were screaming. This was very frightening to me. After eight hours of labor, my beautiful little girl was delivered. We named her Carol Ann; the Carol was for Carroll Smith, whom became our surrogate father while in Austin. We met him and his wife, Mollie, at the First Methodist Church in Austin. Carol Ann weighed in at six pounds, 14 ounces. I might add she had very strong lungs. Mom Smith rode in the ambulance with mother and baby to our apartment from the hospital.

My sister and her 11 year old son, Tommy, came to Austin and stayed a week to help us with the new baby. In those days, new mothers had to stay in bed two weeks after going home from the hospital. The third night sister was there, I went to sleep with Carol Ann nursing. My milk flowed so fast, she got strangled. Sister yelled for Joe who was upstairs studying. I think he bounded down the stairs in 3 steps, grabbed her by her feet and held her upside down tapping her on the back to help her get her breath. What a fright! When she was three months old, we had to put her on the bottle because I had very painful "caked breasts". She thrived on the bottle.

There was no shopping center or grocery store near us. A very enterprising man bought an old school bus and outfitted it as a rolling grocery store. He had some canned goods, some frozen foods, bread, eggs, etc. He drove around the complex twice a day, so if we missed him in the morning we could catch him in the afternoon. Our milk was delivered by a milkman. All the apts. had old fashioned wooden iceboxes. The drain pan ran over and we had to clean up the floor several times so Joe drilled a hole in the floor and put a drain hose from the icebox through the floor and out into the yard. (Production of all factories was geared toward producing equipment for the War effort so no new refrigerators, washing machines, or cars were available) There was an alley between our back fences so delivery people could use it. Our iceman came faithfully twice a week. All we had to do was leave the card in the backdoor window saying what size block we needed and leave the door unlocked for him.

The following February, a couple moved into an apartment across the sidewalk from us—Lemuel L. and Beth LaRue. I knew Beth at North Texas in Denton. LaRue already had a Business degree and came to U.T. to get his Masters. They had a two year old daughter, Kay. Three apartments north of the Larues were Sandy & Jack Robinson. They had a little boy and girl. Jack became a pharmacist and they moved to Houston after graduation. LaRue became the Comptroller at Texas Women's College in Denton; Edward Veigel was a lawyer in the firm of Boyd, Veigel & Gaye in McKinney, Jimmy Horn stayed in Austin and did private work as a lawyer, Johnny Peacock was a coach and later School Superintendent in Goliad, Texas. My husband, Joe was an honor student at U.T. When he graduated in Jan. of 1950, there were few jobs for Electrical Engineers so we moved to Throckmorton and lived with Mom & Dad while Joe looked for a job.

While we were in school, these couples were our best friends. In the summer we played volleyball at night after our children were in bed. The university furnished the net and balls. After a game, we would have homemade ice cream & cookies. Life was great even if we were POOR!!! Our income was $120.00 for married veteran with wife and child. When I worked I made about $120.00 a month too. I didn't work after Carol Ann was born until she was three. Our rent was $30.00 a month. So you can tell we didn't have much to work with.

Easter of 1948, my brother and his family came to Austin to visit us. On Saturday, we drove to San Antonio to go to the sunken Japanese gardens and the zoo. We have movies of brother and the boys riding an elephant. They left for home Sunday morning. That was a wonderful weekend.

In August of 1948 (during Joe's summer break from school), Mother and sister kept Carol Ann and we went on a camping trip with Lee and Sylvia Griffin. We went to the Grand Canyon, Zion Park in Utah, Yellowstone Park and returned home by way of Garden of the Gods in Colorado. Lee had built a teardrop trailer that he and Sylvia could sleep in. The back had a door that lifted up and we could store our food and cook on a Coleman kerosene stove. We were gone three weeks, saw all these sights, ate well, froze sleeping on cots beside the trailer and spent only $100.00. In Idaho, we camped near the Snake River one night. The next morning, while eating breakfast, a coal burning train came by and blew coal dust all over our food. We had a lot of interesting experiences such as bathing in a hot spring in Idaho. Gasoline was 20 cents a gallon and we only ate one meal out. That was on a Sunday in Zion National Park.

In 1949, Joe's senior year, daddy sold us his old 1939 Chevrolet coupe. When we went home during spring break, Joe painted the car. It really looked good. It was quite a luxury for us to have a car. I think we paid dad $300.00 for it. What a treat not to depend on a neighbor to take us or to ride the bus places we needed to go.

Feb. 17, 1949
3 yr., 3 mos.

My sister and her family came to Austin for the Texas-A&M football game at Thanksgiving. About eleven that morning, sister said she had a migraine headache (she had them often). Naturally she didn't feel like going to the game so she stayed at the apartment and babysat Carol Ann. We enjoyed the game and sister enjoyed having Carol Ann to herself. They left for home Saturday.

For Christmas of 1949 we got a cedar tree and put in our living room. It was beautiful. BUT, after it had been up for several days, I ended up in the hospital with asthmatic pneumonia. It was determined that I was very allergic to the cedar pollen. Joe had accepted a job with the Lower Colorado River Authority. We had found a place to live in Marble Falls BUT, the doctor told Joe that if he wanted me to live, we needed to move out of the cedar belt. They had nothing in the way of medicine for allergies back then.

Joe graduated in January of 1950. Since so many former GIs were graduating, the job market was not good. Our income stopped with the month Joe graduated and we also had to vacate the apartment. Since we had to get out of the cedar belt, we moved to my parents for three months until Joe got a job with West Texas Utilities in Abilene. We were fortunate enough to find a cute "shotgun" rental home just a few blocks from Hardin Simmons. I got a job as secretary to the Registrar at Hardin Simmons. We joined St. Paul's Methodist Church and made some nice friends. I had just learned for sure that I was pregnant and we were so excited that Carol Ann would have a sibling. Lo and behold, we learned that W.T.U. was going to transfer Joe to McCamey, Texas. That would put us another 200 miles further west.

My brother offered to move us. We got our belongings loaded onto the truck late in the afternoon. Brother spent the night with his wife's sister & her husband (Mr. & Mrs. Fred Hughes). Joe, Carol Ann and I spent the night with Kathy and Randall Meador who were in our Sunday school class. During the night they had to take me to the hospital because I was miscarrying again. I had to spend a week in the hospital and then go back to my parents for two weeks. Meanwhile, my mother and sister had come to Abilene and picked up Carol Ann. She and mother loved spoiling her while I was incapacitated. Sister and family had planned a trip to Colorado so they took me and Carol Ann to McCamey. I later learned that Bobby and Tommy pitched such a fit at being "cooped up" in the car they gave up the trip and returned to Throckmorton. Joe was the engineer in charge of the substation. We lived in a 2 bedroom company house. It had big rooms and was much nicer than any place we had lived so far. W.T.U. had a little village of company owned houses for their employees. They had drilled deep-water wells so we had plenty of water. We had no utility bills and I think the rent was $30.00 a month. Some of the neighbors would get together to have picnic suppers and make ice cream frequently. It was a grand way of life—slower than city life. The children played well together. McCamey is located about 50 miles south of Odessa, Texas. We had to go to Odessa to the dentist, to do big grocery shopping, etc.

The Veigels let Sandy come to McCamey and visit with us for a week. Then Ed & Ren drove out to visit. We drove to Balmorrhea (west of McCamey) and went swimming in the huge spring-fed pool. From there, we drove to the Davis Mountains and saw the McDonald Observatory on Mt. Locke. That was an experience we all enjoyed.

After living in McCamey for 6 months, Joe had a job offer from his brother Tom's employer Lee W. McClellan. The name of the company was Process Machine and Tool. Joe gave West Texas Utilities two weeks notice and he went to Ohio while Carol Ann and I went to Throckmorton. We stayed with Mother and Dad until the middle of November at which time we rode the train from Dallas to Cleveland.

Joe met us at the train station. It was huge and beautiful. We went to his parent's home where I met his Father Tom, Brothers Bob and Tom and Tom's wife Leona for the first time. His Mother, Mary, had come to see us in Austin when Carol was about six months old. We lived with his parents three or four months. We celebrated Carol Ann's fourth birthday a few days after arriving in Cleveland by wading through knee-deep snow to the bakery to pick up her birthday cake. This was the BIG SNOW of 1950. Forty two inches in 36 hours—it fell so fast, the streetcars and buses were halted in their tracks. After three days, the men took snow shovels and shoveled snow from the street into the yards. The snow plows were working only the main thoroughfares. The corner grocery supplied the men hot coffee as they worked. The supply trucks couldn't get to the neighborhood stores nor could the men get to work for three days. We have a few feet of movies Joe made at this time. It was an unbelievable situation.

Joe enjoyed his new job, but he worked six days a week and often until 10p.m. When they got contract work in, it had to be done as quickly as possible. The U.S. was in the middle of the Korean War. Joe designed the hydraulic control system for the operation of a grinding machine and a milling machine used in the manufacture of the Walker Bulldog T-41-E1 Tank. These grinding and milling machines were made by Wean Manufacturing Co. for the Cadillac Division of General Motors who had the prime contract to manufacture the tank. Joe's company, Process Machine and Tool was a sub-contractor to Wean Equipment. After working for "Mac" for a year, Joe was offered a job as salesman. He would leave home early Monday morning and return late Friday. Mac said he was his best salesman. He located more business for the company than any of the other salesmen.

While we were still living with Joe's parents, I had another miscarriage. My new Dr. located a floating ovarian cyst that had caused this my fourth miscarriage. Why didn't any of my previous doctors find this problem? Surgery was the next step. This was not fun so far from my own family, but I survived. Mom Jurlina was a vigilant and caring nurse.

In March we finally found a lovely apartment in Parma, Ohio. This was an area near the Cleveland Hopkins International Airport. The area around our two-family home (we lived upstairs) was wooded and very lovely. Mr. & Mrs. Sheets lived downstairs. They drank so much, it smelled like a brewery. We were about 15 miles from Joe's parents and about 10 from his work. On the days I needed the car, I would have to take him to work. We were about a mile from the bus line so that was not too convenient. Bob and Mildred Broz lived across the street. They had two sons. Glen was Carol Ann's age and they had a lot of fun playing together until we decided to move closer to Mom & Pop Jurlina.

After about six months, we found an upstairs apartment in a two family home only a block from Joe's parents. It was a lovely place. We had two bedrooms, a large living room, a big dining room, a big kitchen with room for a breakfast table and chairs. It also had a large butler's pantry. Our washing machine was in the basement. We gave Carol

Ann a Lionel train set for Christmas and Joe set it up in the basement. He put a rope swing up for Carol Ann also. She spent many hours swinging, and playing there when the weather was bad. I remember her swinging and singing Buttons and Bows, a very popular song at the time. We attended Wilson Ave. Methodist Church in Cleveland.

My brother was stricken with colon cancer in 1951. He and his wife went to California and to Mexico looking for a cure. These Doctors proved to be quacks. Finally, he was scheduled for surgery in Dallas at Baylor. His wife had to stay with her sons and continue teaching so I flew in from Cleveland to Dallas and stayed with brother until he was able to go home. When the Dr. left the operating room and came to see the family, he said the cancer had spread so much there was nothing he could do for brother but sew him back up. After 8 days, the family took him home and I flew back to Cleveland.

By April I knew I was pregnant again and I desperately wanted my baby to be born in Texas. I finally talked Joe into moving back to Texas. My father had died of pneumonia and heart failure in March. I thought my mother needed me after my brother became so ill so Carol Ann and I moved to Throckmorton in June. In July, Joe came to Throckmorton, too. He took John R. and Jerry on a little trip to Carlsbad Caverns to get their minds off their sick dad. By this time, brother had been hospitalized in Throckmorton for two months. He was in constant pain; had terrific headaches and had lost much weight. He liked to go for short car rides. He weighed so little, Joe could pick him up in his arms and carry him to the car. The heat was terrific so we didn't get to take him for but three or four short rides. This was before cars had air conditioning. We would keep a wet washcloth on brother's forehead while we were out.

Joe started a new job in Dallas with Texas Power & Light Company in September. Our baby, a son Michael Kenneth, was born October 20, 1952. Michael weighed in at 9lbs. 2 oz. and was 21 inches long. I was in Florence Nightingale, Baylor's maternity hospital, for eight days. The morning after coming home, October 29, I was listening to WBAP radio station when I heard about John Grable's death. He was reported to have been a well thought of cattleman and family man. I couldn't believe none of the family had called me, but they later said they didn't want to worry me as they knew I wasn't able to attend his funeral. My mother came to stay with us for a week following his funeral to help with her new grandson. Mother told me that my brother could not speak or swallow near the end. He was able to blink his eyes once to indicate "yes" and twice for "no" and that was all the communication they had with him at the end. The Dr. said his body weighed about 65 pounds. When he got sick, he weighed 205 pounds. My brother was always my handsome hero whom I loved very much. I still love him and miss him. He worshipped his sons and it is such a shame he didn't live to see the fine Christian men they became. He would have been very proud of them. John and his wife, Beaulah Low are buried in the Throckmorton cemetery. (Photographs of their graves are in the appendix)

In Dallas, we lived at 4022 Walker Street in a duplex. It was nice and we had some lovely neighbors. This area was and is called Chalk Hill. After Mike was born, we started looking for a home to buy. Some small California style homes were being built in Oak Cliff in an area bounded by the railroad, Illinois Avenue and Hampton Road. We loved our new home. It cost $10,500.00. The down payment was $1500.00.

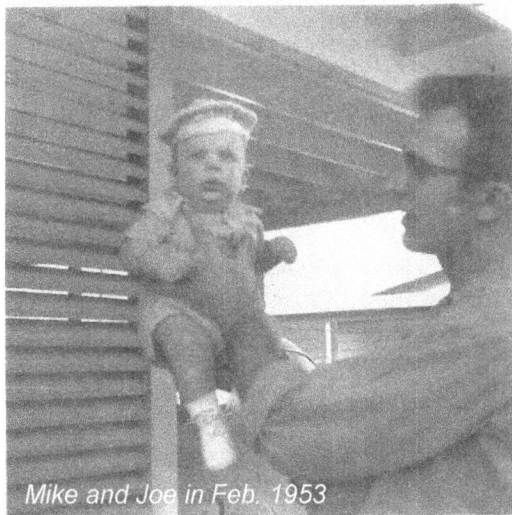
Mike and Joe in Feb. 1953

That was what I inherited from Dad's insurance. We had about a thousand square feet. (3 bedrooms and 1 bath) All the neighbors moved in about the same time. We all had children about the same age so it was great. Joe took an Electrical Engineering job with Texas Power and Light in September of 1952. When Mike was five months old, I had to have a hysterectomy and a lot of repair work done. My mother and my sister kept Mike and Carol Ann for a month while I recovered from the surgery. When they brought Mike home, I couldn't believe it was the same child. He weighed thirty-six pounds. They must have given him a bottle or fed him cereal every time he cried. He was a happy baby who smiled and laughed a lot.

In September of 1953, we enrolled Carol Ann in Lenore Kirk Hall elementary school. It was a new building and she had a lot of good teachers. She was always in advanced classes. She took tap dance lessons and piano lessons. When she entered L.V. Stockard Jr. High, she tried out for the drill team and made it as a Captain.

JOE & JERRY LEE GRABLE AT 2727 WILBUR – JUNE 1956

Our family attended Brooklyn Avenue Methodist Church in Oak Cliff. Joe and I were members of the 50-50 Sunday school class. Mr. A. B. McCann was our teacher. He was one of the most knowledgeable persons of the Bible that I have ever known. We made many wonderful friends in this church. In 1959 Joe (having been reared as a Roman Catholic) said he needed to become a member of a church that had the apostolic succession.

The Episcopal Diocese of Dallas always had a men's Labor Day retreat at their Camp Crucis. Our friend, Ed Veigel of McKinney invited Joe to go to this retreat. While they were at the retreat, the children and I spent the weekend in McKinney with Ren and her children. Dwayne Howell also went with Ed and Joe to the retreat. His wife, Sissy, and Ren spent a lot of the weekend indoctrinating me on the attributes of the Episcopal Church.

When we returned home from the weekend, we had a postcard in our mailbox inviting us to visit St. Georges Episcopal Church in Oak Cliff. We did visit, went to Confirmation classes for nine months (once a week). We were confirmed in January of 1960. The children seemed to like the church as well as we did. After attending church there the first time; I was busy preparing lunch and realized Mike (age 5) was setting up an altar. He had gotten his little wooden stepstool that Joe made for him to reach the bathroom sink, covered it with a dish towel and put two candles on it. He has loved the Episcopal Church since that first visit. He served St. Luke's Episcopal Church as a Vestry member from 2004-2007 and was appointed to be Senior Warden in 2007. Quite a lot was accomplished during that three year period to update and repair the church which is located on Royal Lane just west of Preston Road in Dallas.

Mother suffered a stroke while visiting in our home in 1959. After suffering several mini-strokes, Dr. M.C. Harris admitted her to Methodist Hospital. She was there three months and did not improve any. The hospital administrator called me to his office and told me to look for care for Mother outside the hospital as she was no longer considered a sick person. I called Dr. Nacol in Throckmorton and asked if he would accept mother in the hospital there. He said he would accept her as a patient and make sure she was cared for. Contrary to my sister's wishes, I had mother taken by ambulance to Throckmorton. I guess sister decided to accept the fact that mother was being brought home, because she met the ambulance and us when we pulled into the hospital. We never discussed it further.

After three months, Dr. Harris located a new combination nursing home and hospital in Dallas. It was on Edgefield Drive just south of Davis Street. Sister was about to have a nervous breakdown, so we were happy to learn about this place. In those days, there were very few nursing homes because peoples insurance wouldn't pay for that type of care. This home was smart and had installed a small operating room so it would qualify as a hospital. I moved mother by Merriman's ambulance to Dallas to this home (I can't remember the name of it) in July of 1960. We were able to get a private room across from the nursing station. This way, she could watch the coming and going of people. She could not talk (due to the stroke) so we could understand her. I visited her every day—most days twice a day. When it was warm enough, I would take her outside in a wheelchair so she could see cars go by, watch birds fly, etc. Two days before her seventy second birthday, I asked her what she wanted for her birthday. I thought she said "good will". I said, "Mother, you have everyone's good will". I later realized she had said "GET WELL". She developed pneumonia and passed away peacefully about one p.m. on October 4, 1960. She is buried in Throckmorton alongside her husband, my father. (Death certificates and pictures of their headstones are in appendix.)

Joe's mother became sick in the fall of 1959. At first, the Dr. put her in the hospital in isolation because he thought she had tuberculosis. After many tests, he decided she had lung cancer. In those days, there was no treatment for cancer. They sent her home as they could do nothing for her. She suffered unbearably for about nine months. She passed away June 9, 1960. We have always said she got the cancer from second-hand smoke. Pop Jurlina smoked Lucky Strike cigarettes like they were going out of style.

By this time, Carol Ann was thirteen and Mike was seven. Mike attended the Williamson-Preparatory School for kindergarten. He and Randy Boone were classmates. Randy and baby sister Stacy with their parents Bill and Pat lived across the street from us on Wilbur Street. Mike and Randy were almost inseparable. Where one was, the other had to be. Randy now works for an Episcopal conference center, Kanuga, in Hendersonville, NC, and Stacy is a doctors assistant. Bill died about 20 years ago and Pat had Alzheimer's disease and passed away Nov. 20, 2008.

Joe worked for a year as a Power Consultant in the Central Division of Texas Power & Light. He worked with Fred Willis whom he liked very much. In 1961 Joe had the opportunity to transfer to Sherman as District Manager of the local TP&L office. Our whole family was excited about being in a smaller town, buying a different home, making new friends, and attending a new church (St. Stephens Episcopal). Our second year in Sherman, Joe served 3 years on the vestry and the 3rd year as Jr. Warden. I was the Sunday School Superintendent for St. Stephens. We had some very close friends in Sherman. Loyd Green and his wife Wynnona were special people. Loyd built homes and Wynnona was his decorator for the spec houses. We played bridge and "42" with them a lot. Wynonna introduced me to many of her friends. I was invited to join their birthday group. We would get together at a restaurant near the date of each persons birthday. This continued even after we moved to Richardson. The second Christmas we were in Sherman, Wynnona got me a job for two months at Sears for the Christmas season. I worked with her in the china and gift department.

It was fun but at night my feet hurt so bad and were so sore, I had to soak them in hot salts water for the next day. By the time Christmas Eve arrived, I was so tired I really didn't care if we celebrated Christmas or not..

About 7 or 8 years ago shortly after Loyd died, Wynonna was diagnosed with Parkinsons Disease. We continued to visit and do things with her as long as she was able to use a cane. When she became wheelchair bound, we would take lunch to her home and eat with her every 2 or 3 months. She had to be taken to a nursing home for her last 6 months and recognized friends and loved ones only momentarily. She passed away two years ago and I miss her terribly.

Another close friend was Betsy Kolb. She had two daughters: Diane was Carol Ann's age and Karol was two years older. They attended St. Stephens also. Betsy was a widow and taught first grade at one of the elementary schools. All three of them were artistic, good cooks and a lot of fun. Diane was a bridesmaid in Carol Ann's wedding and so was Carol Ann a bridesmaid for Diane.

The three years we lived in Sherman, I only worked at Christmas that one six week period. I got to "play lady" and play bridge, be in Style Shows, take courses at Austin College, etc. One course I took was speech taught by a Mr. Baird who also went to St. Stephens Church. That course really helped me when I started teaching in Richardson. The company paid for our membership in the Sherman Country Club which was fun. The kids enjoyed the swimming pool and we ate there occasionally. Joe really enjoyed playing golf too.

Carol Ann loved the high school in Sherman. She was Captain of the Drill Team for her Jr. and Sr. years and was in college prep courses. Joe and I were attending the Chamber of Commerce Banquet in April of 1965. We sat with Larry and Mae Krumm. They owned the Chrysler-Plymouth dealership. Part of the entertainment was a style show sponsored by J. C. Penney Co. Carol Ann was one of the models and was very attractive. Mr. Krumm wrote me a note and asked if he could introduce his son, Bill, to our daughter. I saved the note and showed it to Carol Ann. She preserved it as she thought it quite a compliment. In May several Doctors in Sherman would go together and sponsor a Dinner Dance for Senior Girls. Carol Ann did not have a steady boyfriend so I called Mae Krumm and asked her if Bill would be offended to escort Carol Ann to the dinner-dance since he was a college student. So, to make a long story shorter, Bill called Carol Ann for a coke date for a Friday afternoon. He did accompany her to the dance. They had several dates before we were transferred back to Dallas.

When we moved to Richardson, we leased a house for a year. After moving in, we realized Marina Oswald had been living there just before us. It was strange too. News trucks from Channel 5 and 8 would pass by the house slowly as if they could find out something new about the Oswalds. Ordinary citizens would pass by also. It was amazing. We ended up purchasing a home in Estates North on the corner of Mimosa and Seminole Streets (1244 Seminole). We have lived here since July of 1966 and still love the neighborhood. We have seen a lot of people go but the new ones are usually young ones with children who want to attend our good schools and we have a lovely park just a block from us. Joe had to drive to downtown Dallas each day, but three other TP&L'ers rode with him so he had some good conversation time.

After moving to Richardson and since Carol Ann was in College at Tech, we needed a little extra money so I went to work as a secretary at Richardson High School. After the first semester, they needed a study hall keeper so I took that job. I was promoted in the fall of 1967 to teach Home Economics at North Jr. High in the morning and West Jr. High in the afternoon. The following year I was sent to teach at a new Jr. High on Coit Rd. named Northwood. That Jr. High was just about perfect until integration occurred. The black students didn't want to be there. They wanted to keep their own schools and have their own activities. After a couple of years they seemed to adjust somewhat. I had many wonderful students in that school. I stay in contact with several of them which is nice. I remained there six years.

In the fall of 1973 I went back to Richardson High School as the first teacher of H.E.C.E. (Home Economics Coop Education). This was a wonderful way for some students to make decisions for their lifetime role in the world of work. The male students usually worked either in men's fashions or food service as waiters and cooks. I had two young men to go on to Chefs school. The female students worked in fashions, child care, fabric stores, and as waitresses. Many of these students came from broken homes and the money they earned helped their mothers. For me as a teacher, it was the best of two worlds. I was teaching and I was out in the public visiting employers. During this time I attended night classes at North Texas and drove to East Texas State University on Saturdays and obtained my M.S. degree in 1979.

In 1984 The Texas Home Economics Association chose me to be their Teacher of the Year. I competed in The National Teacher of the Year in Anaheim, California. I took all of my credentials to put on display along with teachers from other states. It's been so long I can't remember which state won. It was a good time for all who were in attendance. I went to Calif. 4 days early and took Carol Ann and the two grandchildren. We went to Disneyland and other places of interest which included seeing Howard Hughes plane The Spruce Goose. It is the largest plane ever built at 218 ft., 6in. long with a wing span of 320 ft. and a height of over 79 ft. It could hold over 16,000 gallons of fuel. It is now located in The Spruce Goose Museum in McMinnville, Oregon. I am happy to know it has been preserved for more people to see. The kids returned to Texas and I went to my meeting.

Now, back to the story of Bill and Carol Ann. In January, Bill left for Viet Nam. During the year he was gone, she was attending college at Texas Tech. I think they corresponded almost daily. When he returned to the states, he was stationed in Kansas. Carol Ann transferred to North Texas State University (majoring in Foods and Nutrition). She wanted to be closer to Sherman so she could see Bill when he came home on leave. They became engaged and were married March 9, 1968 at Church of the Transfiguration in Dallas. Fr. James Niles performed the ceremony. After a short honeymoon to Austin, they returned to Kansas to live until his tour of duty was over. Carol Ann got a job as nutritionist at a small hospital in Lawrence, Kansas.

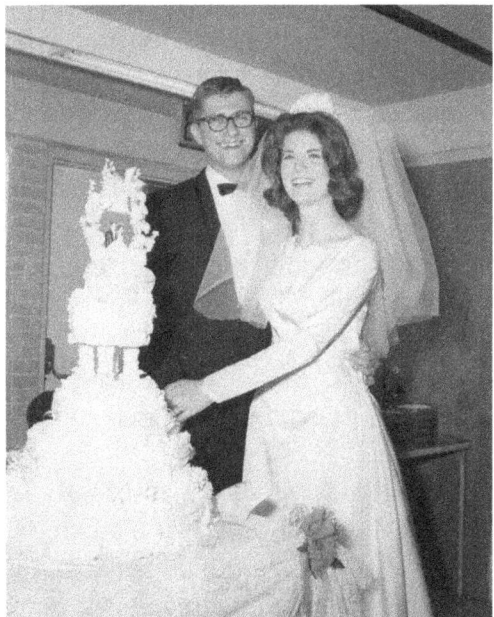

When Bill was separated from the army, they moved to Denton where both entered college. Carol Ann completed her Food and Nutrition

Degree and Bill majored in business. After graduation, they moved to Dallas. They built a home on a private cul-de-sac in Richardson in 1972 where they still reside. They do not want to give up their creek lot and are just about a mile from us which we have enjoyed over the years. When their children were in grade school, junior high and high school at J.J.Pearce, Joe and I knew their friends and enjoyed attending all their school activities.

Carol Ann entered the Registered Dietician program at Parkland Hospital and completed the program with flying colors. She has worked for Presbyterian Hospital, Medical City Hospital, and when her children were young she worked for The Jewish Home for the Aged. She has worked for Baylor Hospital in their Plus 65 program for Senior Citizens which includes her specialty of Diabetes for over 15 years and doesn't seem inclined to retire anytime soon.

Michael enjoyed life in Sherman. He was in the accelerated program the three years we were there. When we moved to Richardson Mike entered the 7th grade at West Jr. High School. He played basketball in the 8th and 9th grade. He was in the choir too. He loved singing and still has a great voice (he sings in our church choir).While in high school, he tried out for football but broke his collarbone and had to forego football. He was in the high school choir. The choir was so great they had Christmas records cut his Jr. and Sr. years which they sold to the public. We have enjoyed them over the years. Mike graduated from high school in May 1971. After much deliberation, he chose to attend college at Baylor. He had saved enough money from working while in high school to pay his tuition. He signed up for the R.O.T.C. program and enjoyed it too much. When he came home for Thanksgiving he told us he was quitting school in January and going into the U.S. Army Infantry. Naturally, Joe and I were very disappointed, but as things have worked out, he has had equally as much if not better education than he would have had in college. After completing basic training at Ft. Polk, Louisiana, he was sent to Washington, D.C. as a member of the Old Guard. His training officer that sent him to D.C. said "You are tall, thin, good looking and smart". He did fit right in with all the Pomp and Circumstance in Washington. His unit was in the funeral parade when President Lyndon Johnson died. They also played a prominent part at the inauguration of President Richard Nixon and many other Official Performances.

After two years he tired of this role and applied to become a Warrant Officer and Helicopter pilot. His Commanding Officer wrote a glowing report which helped him get into the school. He was sent to Fort Wolters, near Mineral Wells, Texas as a member of the last class to train there. Upon graduation, Mike was sent to Germany for three years. He really enjoyed this tour of duty, but after three years he realized the army didn't hold much future for him. He was separated from the army in March of 1977. Joe and I went to Germany and spent Christmas of 1976 with Mike. We got to meet many of his friends, with several of whom he still stays in contact. We got to see and buy trinkets at the Kriskindal Mart. We visited the Albert Durer home and museum. That was interesting. Mike took some leave and drove us from Neuremberg to Munich, to Garmisch, to Innsbrook then to Elmau, Austria. It was Christmas Eve and everything was closed. We finally were able to find a room (the last one) in Elmau. Snow was about three feet deep along the road. About eleven p.m. we left the hotel to go to midnight mass. People were walking along the road all the way (about a mile) to the church. There were candles lighted on every grave in the church graveyard. It was a beautiful sight. The church was full to overflowing. It was freezing in the church. The only heat was a small electric heater directed on the organist. I was wearing insulated underwear, wool slacks and sweater and my wool lined raincoat and was shivering. The service was in German so we couldn't understand what was being said. At midnight, the trumpets joined the organist in playing SILENT NIGHT. It was so beautiful, I felt like we must be close to heaven. After leaving Elmau, we went to Vienna. That is a beautiful place. We then headed back to Neuremberg. We attended an organ concert in a large Lutheran church in downtown Neuremberg. It was beautiful, but cold inside the church.

Mike got a job as a Civilian Instructor at Fort Rucker, Alabama teaching young men to fly helicopters. He took fixed wing lessons while there and earned his pilots license. This took him almost a year. He got a job in Dallas flying for Cohlmia out of Love Field. This gentleman had a contract to fly canceled checks to various Federal Reserve Banks. (This was before computers) Mike and I both paid his "dues" that spring. We had the worst thunderstorms imaginable that spring. His plane had no radar so he would follow airliners into airports. The good Lord watched over him as his mother prayed for his safety.

Once he had built up his fixed wing flying hours, Mike got a job with Buddy Schoelkoff, husband of Caroline Hunt. He would fly them to their entertainment home occasionally in their private plane as well as fly their helicopters. All aircraft was painted orange as the company name was "Pumpkin Air".

After working for Buddy for two years, he got a job with TXI. This was an interesting job as he flew Trammel Crow all over the world to visit his hotels and check on his business endeavors. In 1982 Mike got a job as co-pilot on a twin engine citation jet. The pilot was Hal Chase, a furloughed pilot from American Airlines. The owner was Ed Cox, Jr. Mike really enjoyed this job. He and Hal flew together for three years.

In 1983, Mike was hospitalized at Medical City for an internal bleeding problem. While hospitalized, he met a lovely nurse, Pamela Hasty. Thus the romance began. Meanwhile Hal was called back to American. Following Mike's recovery, Hal told Mike they needed pilots and he should apply. He did and was hired in 1984 as an engineer. (Hal was a great friend—he died of cancer in 1997 after only 5 months of illness). Mike flew to his parent's home to visit with him, had a nice visit and his parents called to tell Mike he had passed away right after he left.

Mike and Pam were married on May 10, 1986. We flew to Massachusetts with Mike and Pam in October of that year to see the leaves. We rented a car and drove through parts of New Hampshire and Vermont. It was a lovely trip. After returning, Mike and Pam bought their first home in Plano. We were happy to have them so close. In 1993, they built a two story home of Austin Stone at 7023 Winding Creek Road, Dallas. Their creek lot is lovely, but the best part is they are only three miles west of us.

We are fortunate to have four lovely grandchildren: Jason Wm. Krumm b. June 30, 1973, Katherine Allison Krumm b. June 18, 1976, Jacob Jarrett Jurlina b. July 13, 1987, and Sabrina Nicole Jurlina b. February 15, 1991. We also have 4 beautiful great-grand children, They all belong to Katherine and Ryan Clark who were married June 6, 1998. They are: Hope Katherine b. February 21, 2000, Anastasia Noelle b. January 10, 2002, Josiah Michael b. December 8, 2004 and Joshua Ryan b. March 30, 2007.

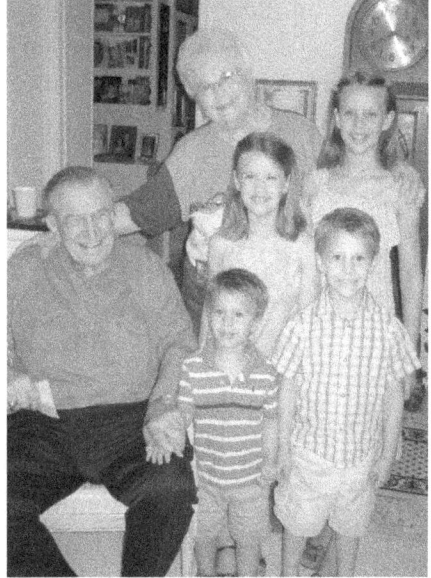

Jason is a registered Professional Architect working in Chicago for Newman Architects after spending three years working in Minneapolis. Jason's girlfriend, Jennie English is a Lutheran Minister in the Chicago area. Katherine has her Masters Degree from Wheaton College in Ill. She is home schooling Hope, Anya, and Josiah. Katherine's husband Ryan is a Lutheran Minister in Walden, New York; they seem to like it there. Jacob is a college senior majoring in business at Southern Methodist University. He did an internship in Houston last summer for JP Morgan Co. Sabrina graduated from Parish Episcopal School this spring (2009). She played basketball, ran track in high school, as well as singing and playing the piano like a professional. (She was honored to compete at the state piano competition two years in a row!) Sabrina models for Campbell Modeling Co. She has just begun her freshman year at TCU in Fort Worth double majoring in Business and Music.

Our grandchildren at Sabrina's graduation; Jacob, Jason, Sabrina, and Katherine

While Joe and I were still working, we made two trips to England, the first in 1982 and the second in 1985. In the appendix, you can enjoy my daily diary of these two (and other) trips. JoAnn Bell, our Richardson School System Library Consultant, and a dedicated Anglophile had made many trips to England and took 5 to 7 people interested in discovering their English roots. We had not started our quest for my family history at that time or I could probably have learned some valuable information at Kings Lynn. Several years later we learned that our Joseph Vick had left Kings Lynn in the 1660's to come to the United States as an indentured servant settling in Isle of Wight, Va. We spent the night there and walked around the small village the next morning. Maybe my short story will encourage you to learn more about your ancestors while traveling.

We both retired in 1987. Since we had enjoyed traveling with Rev. Lee Griffin and his wife 39 years earlier, we invited them to travel with us to Nova Scotia. As a retirement gift to ourselves, we bought a beautiful two-tone grey suburban to travel in. The Griffins had a former parishioner from their Methodist church in Corpus Christi living in Round Pond, Maine that they wanted to visit. After spending part of a day and night with Joe's army buddy, Ed Mooridian in New York, we went on to Maine. That part of our U.S.A. is indescribably beautiful. If you haven't been there, you must go. Nova Scotia proved to be a beautiful area where the people were very friendly. Their Canadian Province had a wonderful way to help tourists find rooms for the night. People who wanted to let rooms for the night were registered in a travel booklet so we would call each morning to a place where we wanted to stay that night and request a room. We met many lovely people and enjoyed the beauty of their cities as well as the countryside.

We experienced our first trip with Lee and Sylvia to Yellowstone and 40 years later we were able to experience this trip to Nova Scotia with them. GOD is GOOD!!! and FRIENDS are WONDERFUL.

We became involved in family research after our return from this trip. We made a visit to the Museum Courthouse in Vicksburg, MS in 1982. We were told about a Vick Family organization and upon contacting the lady in charge, we were invited to the next reunion. We really enjoyed the cousins we met so from 1984 until 1999 we attended all of the reunions but two. The reunions were held in June. We met many new relatives at each reunion and renewed acquaintances with others.

We would meet Friday until Sunday, have a program speaker, do tours of the area especially in the areas where our forbears had lived, and shared family information.

My cousin, Mary Jo McCary who started the reunions, helped James Perrin write a quarterly newsletter and mailed it to the members. These were invaluable because they contained so much VICK information. By attending our second reunion in Vicksburg, we found many cousins who were direct descendants of my great-grandfather, Isaiah Vick. My grandfather, Nathan Monroe, was Isaiah's son by his third wife. Nathan married Mary Elizabeth Lopp of Keller, Texas. Vicksburg was named in honor of the Vicks who lived there and fought in the Civil War. Newit Vick had a huge plantation northeast of downtown Vicksburg. Newit and his wife and some of their children are buried in a small park in a corner of the plantation.

Mary Jo became ill in 1992 with a brain tumor. When she became ill, she called and asked Joe and me to take over the printing and mailing of the newsletter. By this time, John Beatty of Ft. Wayne was authoring our newsletter. Because of John's work constraints, he had to give up writing the newsletter so DiAnn Vick took on that responsibility. Joe and I printed and mailed the newsletter for seven years in addition to keeping the financial records and recording new members. John is the director of the Genealogy section of the Fort Wayne Library. Subsequently, John and DiAnn Vick wrote our recently published family book—JOSEPH VICK of Lower Parish, Isle of Wight County, Virginia and his descendants. The book contains information about the first five generations of Vicks in the U.S.A. Mary Jo died in 1994. She has truly been missed. Shortly after her death, our wonderful cousin Richard Wright (he is a lawyer in N.C.) incorporated The Joseph Vick Family of America in North Carolina. DiAnn did a magnificent job until her health and the writing and publishing of the Vick book slowed her down. Our last newsletter was received in 2007 which was for the third and fourth quarter of 2003. We look forward to more soon.

Some of our younger Vick men are participating in DNA projects trying to prove their lineage. Too bad only males with surname of Vick can verify the lineage. My Vick grandparents only had (7) daughters. One of the young men, Larry Vick, is a great-grandson of Stephen who is my great-grandfathers brother. He has proved through his DNA testing that our great-grandfathers truly were brothers. (Nov. 7, '07--The relationship has now been proven by a male cousin of DiAnn Vick.) While we were so active in the Vick Family Organization, we attended several three day reunions as follows:

1988---Isle of Wight, Virginia	1994---Franklin, Virginia
1989---Vicksburg, MS.	1995---Paducah, Kentucky
1990---Franklin, Virginia	1996---Portsmouth, Virginia
1991---Charlotte, N. Carolina	1997---Vicksburg, MS
1992---Selma, Alabama	1999---Fort Wayne, Indiana

We usually spent three or four days before and after the reunion seeing places and doing more family research. It was great meeting new people and breaking bread with them.

My father's family information (GRABLE) has been obtained mostly from cousins who have done research: Maxine Grable Cherryhomes (my first cousin) of Jacksboro, TX hired several professional genealogists and had information from the 1600s which she shared with me. A family pedigree chart is in the back of this book (Appendix A). Evelyn Smith Hill Vogel of Ft. Worth and Archie Elmo Grable both of Ft. Worth have shared family information with me. Elmo gave me copies of articles that appeared in the Chicago Tribune on Sunday, August 21, 1930 of my father's brother, Virgil known as "Victor" who was a band leader in Chicago. He was an associate of John Philip Sousa at Great Lakes Training Station during WWI.

Victor Grable

"Mr. Grable was one of the first bandleaders to cross the ocean with the American forces. The article in the Chicago Tribune was about The Chicagoland Music Festival. Three times it broke the world's record of 100 thousand attendance established by the meeting of the International Choral Union of Vienna in 1929. The greatest throng ever to attend the Festival greatly exceeded the capacity of

Soldiers Field when 150 thousand people filled every seat, and every inch of standing room; while 30 thousand people were turned away. The success of these festivals is credited to the musical ability of Victor Grable. Conductor Grable, who was discovered by John Philip Sousa, and energetically promoted by him, has been a leader in the development of high school bands throughout the country through the medium of contests starting in 1922." (A copy of The Chicago Tribune article is in the appendix.)

I sent the articles about Uncle Victor to The University of Maryland Performing Arts Library plus an original photograph in his band uniform. They placed these items in their American Bandmasters Association Research Center.

Mike, Pam, Jacob (age 3), Joe, and I flew to Hawaii, the Island of Maui for 6 days in 1990. It rained some every day we were there; therefore the guys did not get to play golf as planned. We did have some time in the sun where Joe and I sat on the beach and watched the whales coming in. We had a two bedroom, bath and kitchen apartment at the Kallipali Resort. Our balcony on the 7th floor overlooked the beautifully landscaped grounds, the pool and the ocean. Every time we got in the car to go somewhere Jacob would sing "I've Been Working on the Railroad" until he fell asleep. One day, we did ride the Cane Train which was interesting. On Sunday we attended an Episcopal church. Jacob enjoyed the Sunday School and children. We loved all the scenery in Maui, but the 14 hour trip back home almost did me in. I slept 10 hours straight after arriving home.

ROYAL VIKING LINE   /991   ROYAL VIKING SKY

Our dear friends, Glenie and Jim Byron (now deceased), invited us to go on an Alaskan Cruise with them in 1991. We sailed on The Royal Viking Sky. It was a small ship holding only 650 passengers. We took several day trips onto the mainland which were great. We saw much beautiful country as well as lots of wildlife on the day trips. We cruised from Vancouver to Juneau. We took a driving tour of Juneau and visited two museums. Later we took a helicopter ride out over the glacier field. The lady pilot landed and we walked out over a small portion of the glacier. The crevices we observed were very, very deep. I would hate to fall into one because recovery would be difficult. We boarded our ship, The Royal Viking Sky, and cruised up the coast to Sitka. It is formerly a Russian town and still has a lot of Russian influence in the decorations of the churches, etc. I purchased a necklace at The Jeweler's Bench which cost $64.00 and a bracelet that cost $22.00. The stones are called "Arctic-Opal" and are a dark blue with green specks in them. We had been told to return to our ship by 6 p.m. sharp. There were two women that were always late. The ship set sail without them, but before we cleared the harbor, here came a small boat roaring up alongside our ship with the two women. A rope ladder was lowered for them to come aboard, but they didn't have the strength to make it alone so the sailors had to push them up by their bottoms. Believe me they were not late again. The Captain made believers of them that time.

We had never been on a cruise before and this one proved to be great. Each night a newsletter of 6 to 8 pages was left under our door giving a schedule of activities for the next day plus off-ship trips available to us. The ship had a swimming pool, a miniature golf place, shuffleboard, table tennis, bridge, dominoes, slot machines, an exercise room and a small library. In the evening we dressed formally, had dinner, did some ballroom dancing and then were entertained by young people performing a Broadway type show. They had a movie theatre and on Sunday used it for an informal church service. They provided square dance lessons. At teatime, we were entertained by a harpist. We took a bus tour into Anchorage. They had several of the same department stores we have. I purchased a pair of Arctic Opal earrings in a large department store to wear with the necklace. The town was lovely. They had huge blooming baskets hanging all over downtown. The only bad thing was seeing so many of the natives lying in public places drunk. I understood this was one of Alaska's largest problems due to unemployment. Returning from Anchorage, we stopped at The Boggs Visitor Center to see a film and view The Portage Glacier. We sailed to

Victoria and visited the Buchart Gardens. The last day we sailed into Vancouver and bid our ship and shipmates farewell.

Upon our arrival in Vancouver, our hotel rooms were not ready to be occupied so they took us to the ballrooms for cokes and chips. I wandered down to the first floor to visit the gift shop. (This trip was made during the Desert Storm Conflict.) The young clerk and I started talking. She asked if I saw many yellow ribbons around the trees in Anchorage. I told her they were everywhere. She said her family came to Canada from Croatia and she and her brothers wanted to return to help the Croatians fight against the Serbs, but their parents wouldn't hear of it. I told her my father-in-law came to the states from Croatia in 1913. She inquired about our name and when I told her it was Jurlina, she exclaimed—"My God, I went to High School with a girl whose last name was Jurlina". I ran back to the ballroom and brought Joe to talk to the young lady. She gave him the girl's father's name. Joe called their home and talked to Mira, Milan's wife. He was in Croatia at the time with two of his sons building a home over there. After much conversation, it was determined Joe and Milan were cousins. After returning home, and many phone conversations with them, we set a date to visit their family compound in Croatia.

In 2001, Mike and his family and Joe and I left June 24 from DFW on a 777 airliner for Zurich, Switzerland. We had a 4 hour wait before flying on to Zagreb, Croatia so we toured the airport. It is a small city within the airport with all kinds of beautiful shops. We boarded a small Swiss Air plane to Zagreb. We were like sardines in a can. We met many Jurlinas in Croatia where Joe's father, Tom, was born. We spent time in Zadar and Zagreb and ended up in Selena. We stayed with a cousins wife in their home located about 75 feet from the Adriatic Sea and only about a mile from the Velebit Mountains (part of the Alps). We made a day trip into Slovenia where Joe's maternal grandmother was born. The countryside in Slovenia is very beautiful. Joe was unable to get much family information except by word of mouth from two cousins. (The trips diary is in the appendix.)

Our next family trip was in 2004. Since Joe is such a whiz on the computer, he located a Michael Jurlina, an outstanding salesman of real estate, in New Zealand in 2004. So, of course, he had to e-mail him. Sure enough his grandfather had left Croatia and gone to New Zealand in the late 1800's. With this information, we planned a trip to the North

Island of New Zealand to meet more relatives. Pamela is the family "expert" in the traveling area, so she made all the flying, hotel, and van rental arrangements. This trip was our most extensive family trip to meet more of Joe's cousins.

I must say we were entertained royally while visiting in their communities. We were in New Zealand 12 days, met about 35 Jurlinas and had a most wonderful time. Mike, Pam and the children got to go to a Rugby game. Joe and I watched it on TV at the hotel. Aukland is a big city and very pretty. We did a lot of sightseeing there. In the town of Rotorua, we enjoyed the sights, the children did rockclimbing, etc. The last evening there, we had dinner at "THE LONE STAR CAFE". They said it had no connection to Texas. We still stay in contact with the relatives.

In 1995 we went on a bus tour from Calgary, Canada up to Montana and back to Calgary. Our friends, the Parrs and Veigels were on this trip. A friend of ours has a time share at Beaver Creek, CO. We have been there with him and his wife (Bob and Tiny Anderson). Tiny died about five years ago of cancer. Bob has loaned it to Mike and his family and us two different times. It is a glorious place.

Our life has been a good one. God has blessed us in so many ways. We have worked hard and have a great family. Our children and grandchildren had celebrations for our 40th, 50th and 60th wedding anniversaries. (The newspaper write-up from the 60th anniversary is in the appendix.) Each of the parties was well attended and have left us with many memories. We are halfway to our 63rd anniversary at this writing. We are active in our St. Luke's Episcopal Church on Royal Lane at Preston in Dallas. We have been members of the Kermis Dance Club because we love ballroom dancing; however we have reached the age that once or twice around the floor is all we can make. Joe is a member of the Texas State Professional Engineers (T.S.P.E.) and I have been active in the auxiliary for 22 years. I am also active in the Richardson Retired Teachers Association.

We look forward to the time we have left and by going to our YMCA three times a week are trying to stay physically active and healthy.

Many thanks go to my husband, Joe, and my children for their encouragement in getting this little book completed. My husband who is not always patient, has been most patient in helping me master (almost) the use of my computer. I could never have accomplished this task without his help.

I also want to thank my lovely granddaughter Katherine Krumm Clark for inserting the photographs and the other information into the book and arranging the printing for me.

I hope each of my relatives who read this will learn more about your mother, grandmother, aunt, cousin, friend, and whatever other relation I am to you.

Love to each one,

Billie John (Grable) Jurlina

Family picture taken at the 60th Anniversary party- Mike's family on the left, Carol Ann and Bill, center, Ryan and Katherine and their children next, then Jason on the right.

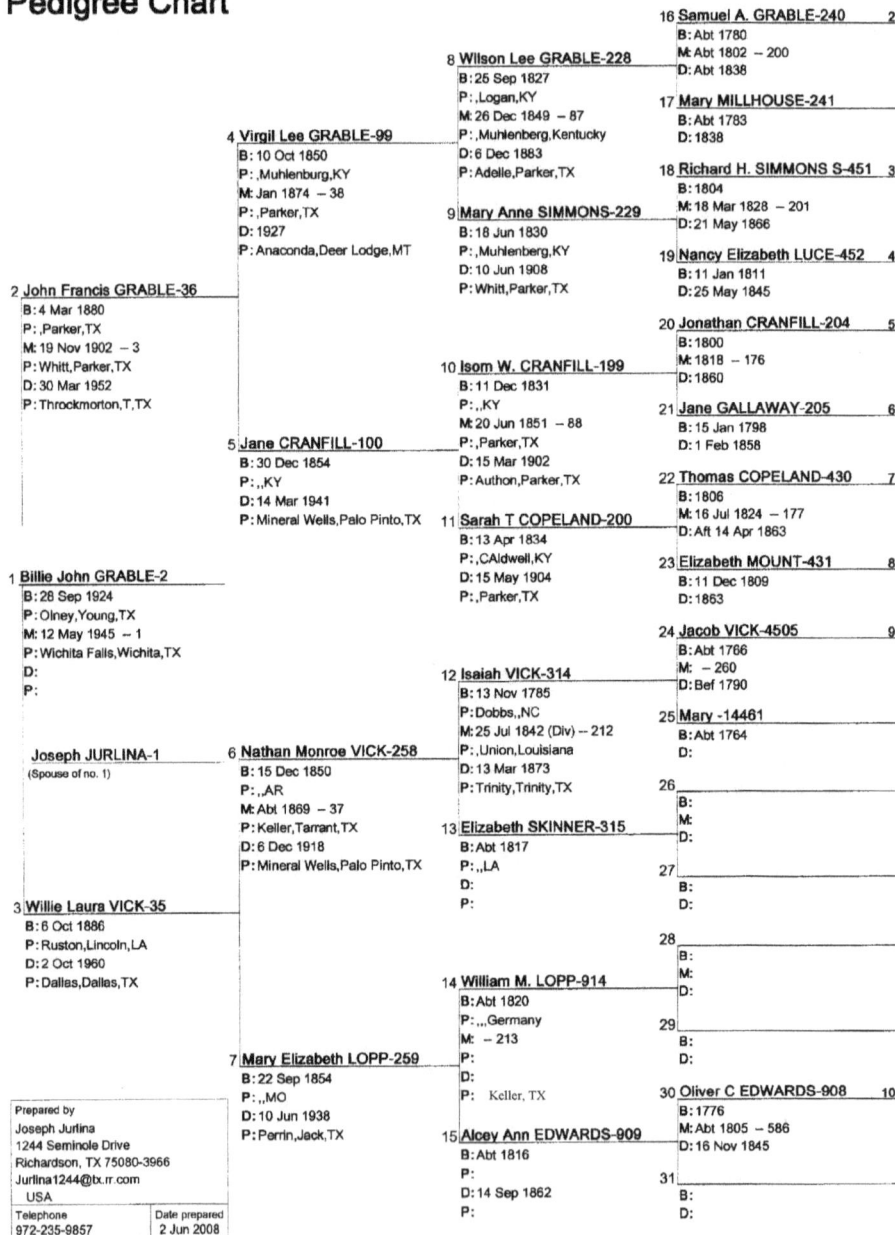

Appendix A:
Pedigree Charts

Pedigree Chart

16 Samuel A. GRABLE-240   **2**
B: Abt 1780
M: Abt 1802 – 200
D: Abt 1838

8 Wilson Lee GRABLE-228
B: 25 Sep 1827
P: ,Logan,KY
M: 26 Dec 1849 – 87
P: ,Muhlenberg,Kentucky
D: 6 Dec 1883
P: Adelle,Parker,TX

17 Mary MILLHOUSE-241
B: Abt 1783
D: 1838

4 Virgil Lee GRABLE-99
B: 10 Oct 1850
P: ,Muhlenburg,KY
M: Jan 1874 – 38
P: ,Parker,TX
D: 1927
P: Anaconda,Deer Lodge,MT

18 Richard H. SIMMONS S-451   **3**
B: 1804
M: 18 Mar 1828 – 201
D: 21 May 1866

9 Mary Anne SIMMONS-229
B: 18 Jun 1830
P: ,Muhlenberg,KY
D: 10 Jun 1908
P: Whitt,Parker,TX

19 Nancy Elizabeth LUCE-452   **4**
B: 11 Jan 1811
D: 25 May 1845

2 John Francis GRABLE-36
B: 4 Mar 1880
P: ,Parker,TX
M: 19 Nov 1902 – 3
P: Whitt,Parker,TX
D: 30 Mar 1952
P: Throckmorton,T,TX

20 Jonathan CRANFILL-204   **5**
B: 1800
M: 1818 – 176
D: 1860

10 Isom W. CRANFILL-199
B: 11 Dec 1831
P: ,,KY
M: 20 Jun 1851 – 88
P: ,Parker,TX
D: 15 Mar 1902
P: Authon,Parker,TX

21 Jane GALLAWAY-205   **6**
B: 15 Jan 1798
D: 1 Feb 1858

5 Jane CRANFILL-100
B: 30 Dec 1854
P: ,,KY
D: 14 Mar 1941
P: Mineral Wells,Palo Pinto,TX

22 Thomas COPELAND-430   **7**
B: 1806
M: 16 Jul 1824 – 177
D: Aft 14 Apr 1863

11 Sarah T COPELAND-200
B: 13 Apr 1834
P: ,CAldwell,KY
D: 15 May 1904
P: ,Parker,TX

23 Elizabeth MOUNT-431   **8**
B: 11 Dec 1809
D: 1863

1 Billie John GRABLE-2
B: 28 Sep 1924
P: Olney,Young,TX
M: 12 May 1945 – 1
P: Wichita Falls,Wichita,TX
D:
P:

24 Jacob VICK-4505   **9**
B: Abt 1766
M: – 260
D: Bef 1790

12 Isaiah VICK-314
B: 13 Nov 1785
P: Dobbs,,NC
M: 25 Jul 1842 (Div) – 212
P: ,Union,Louisiana
D: 13 Mar 1873
P: Trinity,Trinity,TX

25 Mary -14461
B: Abt 1764
D:

Joseph JURLINA-1
(Spouse of no. 1)

6 Nathan Monroe VICK-258
B: 15 Dec 1850
P: ,,AR
M: Abt 1869 – 37
P: Keller,Tarrant,TX
D: 6 Dec 1918
P: Mineral Wells,Palo Pinto,TX

13 Elizabeth SKINNER-315
B: Abt 1817
P: ,,LA
D:
P:

26
B:
M:
D:

27
B:
D:

3 Willie Laura VICK-35
B: 6 Oct 1886
P: Ruston,Lincoln,LA
D: 2 Oct 1960
P: Dallas,Dallas,TX

28
B:
M:
D:

14 William M. LOPP-914
B: Abt 1820
P: ,,,Germany
M: – 213
P:
P: Keller, TX

29
B:
D:

7 Mary Elizabeth LOPP-259
B: 22 Sep 1854
P: ,,MO
D: 10 Jun 1938
P: Perrin,Jack,TX

30 Oliver C EDWARDS-908   **10**
B: 1776
M: Abt 1805 – 586
D: 16 Nov 1845

15 Alcey Ann EDWARDS-909
B: Abt 1816
P:
D: 14 Sep 1862
P:

31
B:
D:

Prepared by
Joseph Jurlina
1244 Seminole Drive
Richardson, TX 75080-3966
Jurlina1244@tx.rr.com
USA

Telephone	Date prepared
972-235-9857	2 Jun 2008

60

Pedigree Chart

No. 1 on this chart is the same as no. 16 on chart no. 1

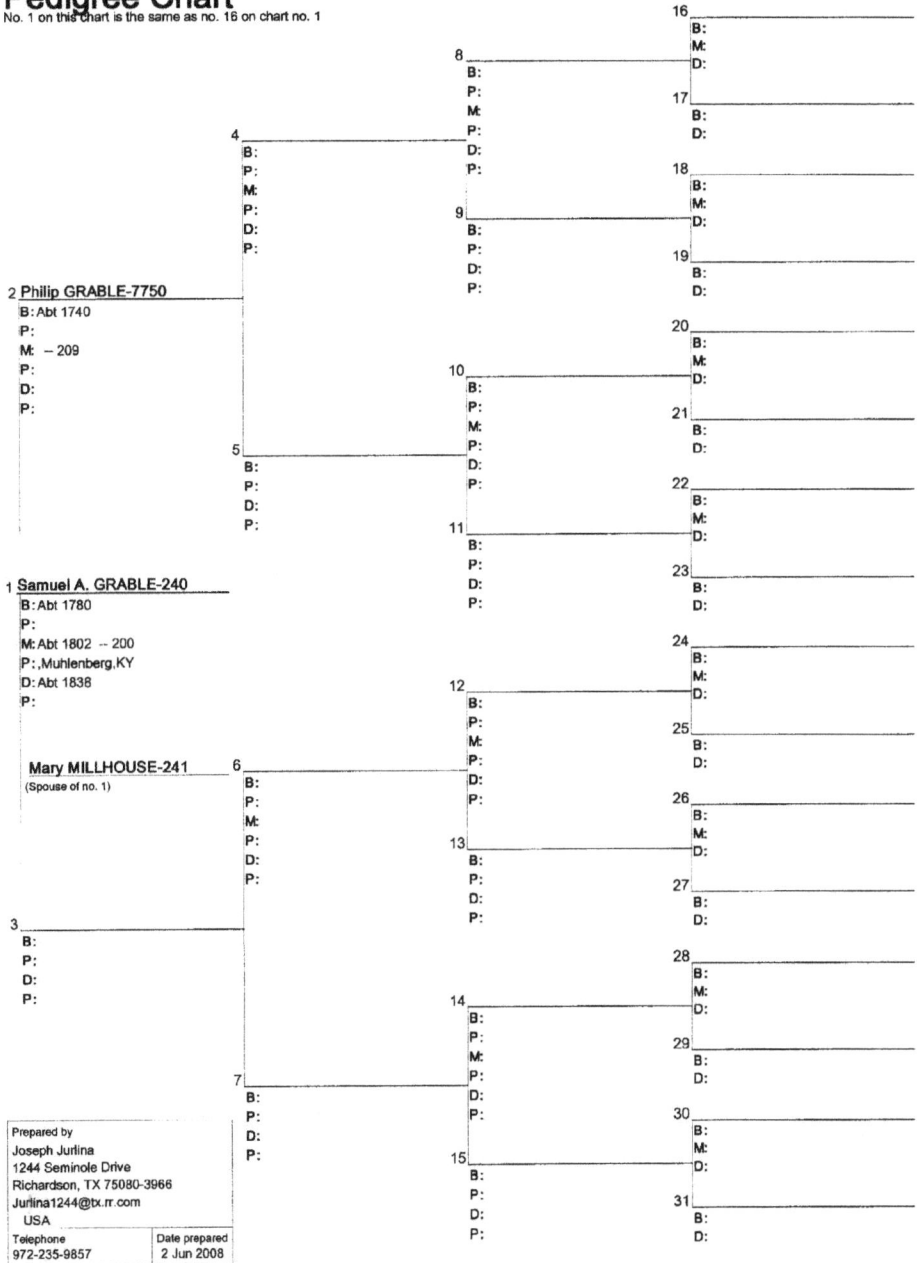

```
                                                            16 _____
                                                               B:
                                                               M:
                                          8 _____    D:
                                            B:
                                            P:               17 _____
                                            M:                  B:
                 4 _____     P:                  D:
                   B:                       P:
                   P:                       D:               18 _____
                   M:                       P:                  B:
                   P:                                           M:
                   D:                     9 _____    D:
                   P:                       B:
                                            P:               19 _____
                                            D:                  B:
  2 Philip GRABLE-7750                      P:                  D:
    B: Abt 1740
    P:                                                       20 _____
    M: - 209                                                    B:
    P:                                   10 _____    M:
    D:                                      B:                  D:
    P:                                      P:
                                            M:               21 _____
                                            P:                  B:
                 5 _____     D:                  D:
                   B:                       P:
                   P:                                        22 _____
                   D:                                           B:
                   P:                    11 _____    M:
                                            B:                  D:
                                            P:
  1 Samuel A. GRABLE-240                    D:               23 _____
    B: Abt 1780                             P:                  B:
    P:                                                          D:
    M: Abt 1802 -- 200
    P: ,Muhlenberg,KY                                        24 _____
    D: Abt 1838                                                 B:
    P:                                   12 _____    M:
                                            B:                  D:
                                            P:
                                            M:               25 _____
      Mary MILLHOUSE-241   6 _____   P:                  B:
      (Spouse of no. 1)     B:              P:                  D:
                            P:              D:
                            M:              P:               26 _____
                            P:                                  B:
                            D:                                  M:
                            P:           13 _____    D:
                                            B:
                                            P:               27 _____
                                            D:                  B:
  3 _____                  P:                  D:
    B:
    P:                                                       28 _____
    D:                                                          B:
    P:                                                          M:
                                         14 _____    D:
                                            B:
                                            P:               29 _____
                                            M:                  B:
                 7 _____     P:                  D:
                   B:                       D:
                   P:                       P:               30 _____
                   D:                                           B:
                   P:                    15 _____    M:
                                            B:                  D:
                                            P:
                                            D:               31 _____
                                            P:                  B:
                                                               D:
```

Prepared by
Joseph Jurlina
1244 Seminole Drive
Richardson, TX 75080-3966
Jurlina1244@tx.rr.com
USA

Telephone	Date prepared
972-235-9857	2 Jun 2008

61

Pedigree Chart

No. 1 on this chart is the same as no. 18 on chart no. 1

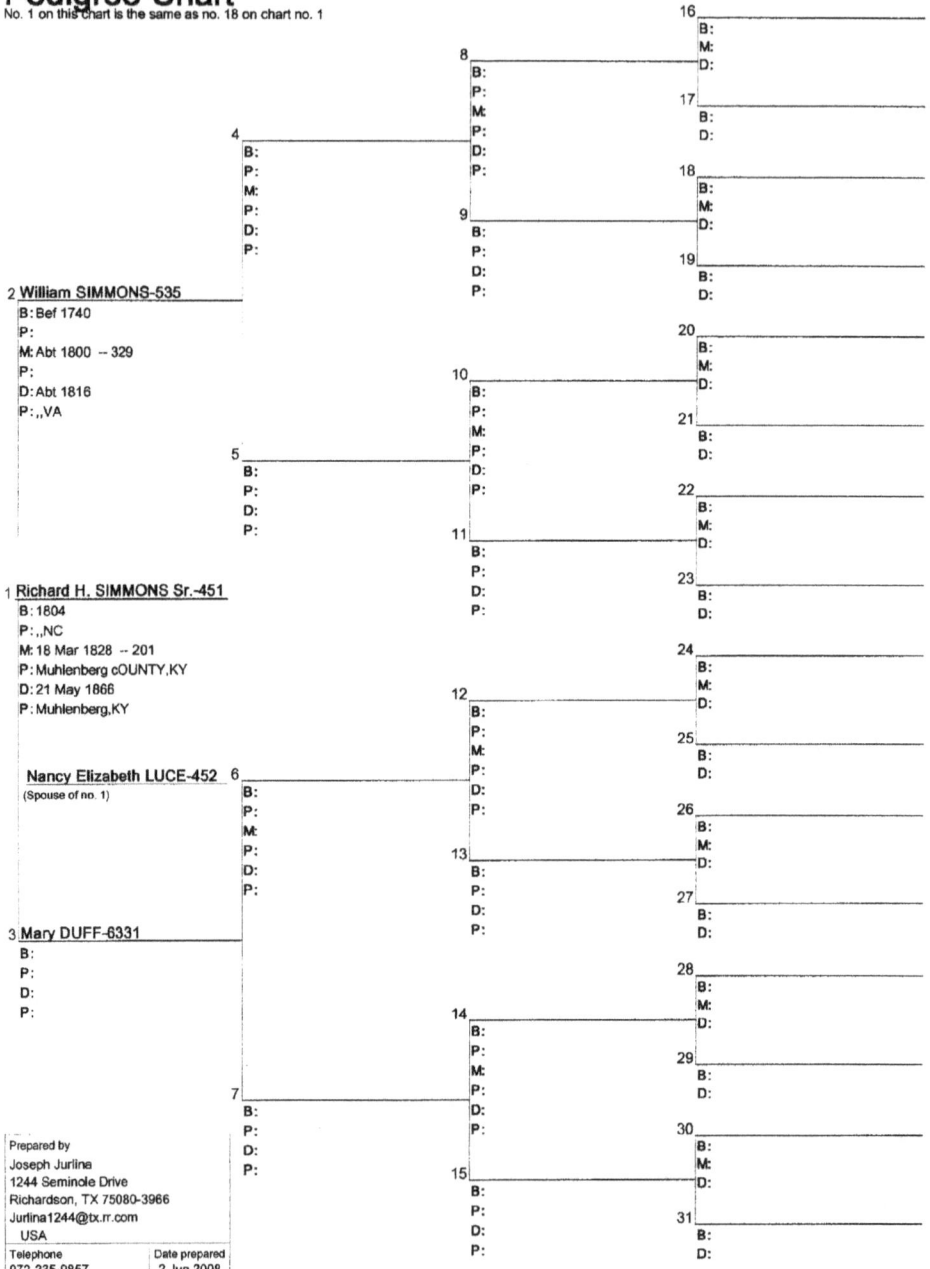

2 William SIMMONS-535
B: Bef 1740
P:
M: Abt 1800 -- 329
P:
D: Abt 1816
P: ,,VA

1 Richard H. SIMMONS Sr.-451
B: 1804
P: ,,NC
M: 18 Mar 1828 -- 201
P: Muhlenberg cOUNTY,KY
D: 21 May 1866
P: Muhlenberg,KY

Nancy Elizabeth LUCE-452 6
(Spouse of no. 1)

3 Mary DUFF-6331
B:
P:
D:
P:

4
B:
P:
M:
P:
D:
P:

5
B:
P:
D:
P:

6
B:
P:
M:
P:
D:
P:

7
B:
P:
D:
P:

8
B:
P:
M:
P:
D:
P:

9
B:
P:
D:
P:

10
B:
P:
M:
P:
D:
P:

11
B:
P:
D:
P:

12
B:
P:
M:
P:
D:
P:

13
B:
P:
D:
P:

14
B:
P:
M:
P:
D:
P:

15
B:
P:
D:
P:

16
B:
M:
D:

17
B:
D:

18
B:
M:
D:

19
B:
D:

20
B:
M:
D:

21
B:
D:

22
B:
M:
D:

23
B:
D:

24
B:
M:
D:

25
B:
D:

26
B:
M:
D:

27
B:
D:

28
B:
M:
D:

29
B:
D:

30
B:
M:
D:

31
B:
D:

Prepared by
Joseph Jurlina
1244 Seminole Drive
Richardson, TX 75080-3966
Jurlina1244@tx.rr.com
USA

Telephone
972-235-9857

Date prepared
2 Jun 2008

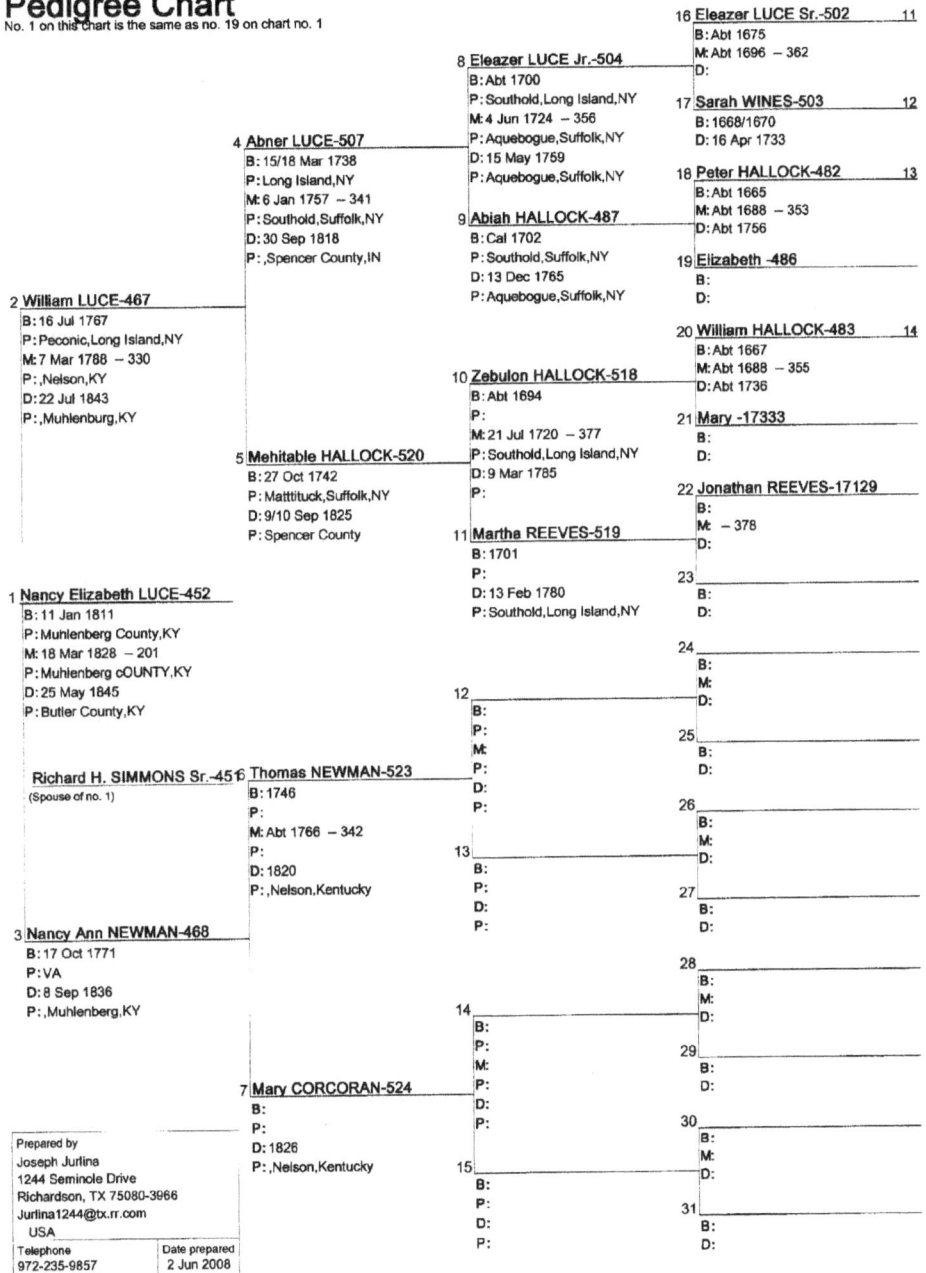

Pedigree Chart

No. 1 on this Chart is the same as no. 19 on chart no. 1

16 Eleazer LUCE Sr.-502 _____11
B: Abt 1675
M: Abt 1696 — 362
D:

17 Sarah WINES-503 _____12
B: 1668/1670
D: 16 Apr 1733

8 Eleazer LUCE Jr.-504
B: Abt 1700
P: Southold, Long Island, NY
M: 4 Jun 1724 — 356
P: Aquebogue, Suffolk, NY
D: 15 May 1759
P: Aquebogue, Suffolk, NY

18 Peter HALLOCK-482 _____13
B: Abt 1665
M: Abt 1688 — 353
D: Abt 1756

19 Elizabeth -486
B:
D:

9 Abiah HALLOCK-487
B: Cal 1702
P: Southold, Suffolk, NY
D: 13 Dec 1765
P: Aquebogue, Suffolk, NY

4 Abner LUCE-507
B: 15/18 Mar 1738
P: Long Island, NY
M: 6 Jan 1757 — 341
P: Southold, Suffolk, NY
D: 30 Sep 1818
P: , Spencer County, IN

20 William HALLOCK-483 _____14
B: Abt 1667
M: Abt 1688 — 355
D: Abt 1736

21 Mary -17333
B:
D:

10 Zebulon HALLOCK-518
B: Abt 1694
P:
M: 21 Jul 1720 — 377
P: Southold, Long Island, NY
D: 9 Mar 1785
P:

22 Jonathan REEVES-17129
B:
M: — 378
D:

23
B:
D:

11 Martha REEVES-519
B: 1701
P:
D: 13 Feb 1780
P: Southold, Long Island, NY

2 William LUCE-467
B: 16 Jul 1767
P: Peconic, Long Island, NY
M: 7 Mar 1788 — 330
P: , Nelson, KY
D: 22 Jul 1843
P: , Muhlenburg, KY

5 Mehitable HALLOCK-520
B: 27 Oct 1742
P: Mattituck, Suffolk, NY
D: 9/10 Sep 1825
P: Spencer County

24
B:
M:
D:

25
B:
D:

12
B:
P:
M:
P:
D:
P:

26
B:
M:
D:

27
B:
D:

13
B:
P:
D:
P:

1 Nancy Elizabeth LUCE-452
B: 11 Jan 1811
P: Muhlenberg County, KY
M: 18 Mar 1828 — 201
P: Muhlenberg cOUNTY, KY
D: 25 May 1845
P: Butler County, KY

6 Thomas NEWMAN-523
B: 1746
P:
M: Abt 1766 — 342
P:
D: 1820
P: , Nelson, Kentucky

28
B:
M:
D:

29
B:
D:

14
B:
P:
M:
P:
D:
P:

30
B:
M:
D:

31
B:
D:

15
B:
P:
D:
P:

Richard H. SIMMONS Sr.-45
(Spouse of no. 1)

3 Nancy Ann NEWMAN-468
B: 17 Oct 1771
P: VA
D: 8 Sep 1836
P: , Muhlenberg, KY

7 Mary CORCORAN-524
B:
P:
D: 1826
P: , Nelson, Kentucky

Prepared by
Joseph Jurlina
1244 Seminole Drive
Richardson, TX 75080-3966
Jurlina1244@tx.rr.com
USA

Telephone
972-235-9857

Date prepared
2 Jun 2008

Pedigree Chart

2 Thomas CRANFILL-213
B: Abt 1770
P:
M: Abt 1797 -- 180
P: ,Rowan,NC
D: Abt 1828
P:

4 Hezekiah CRANFILL-221
B: Abt 1740
P: ,,,England
M: Abt 1769 -- 188
P:
D: Abt 1796
P:

8 CRANFILL-560
B: Abt 1720
P: ,,,England
M: Abt 1769 -- 193
P:
D:
P:

16
B:
M:
D:

17
B:
D:

9
B:
P:
D:
P:

18
B:
M:
D:

19
B:
D:

5 Ann NEEDLES-222
B: Abt 1745
P:
D:
P:

10 NEEDLES-17231
B:
P:
M: -- 194
P:
D:
P:

20
B:
M:
D:

21
B:
D:

11
B:
P:
D:
P:

22
B:
M:
D:

23
B:
D:

1 Jonathan CRANFILL-204
B: 1800
P: ,Rowan,NC
M: 1818 -- 176
P: ,,NC
D: 1860
P: ,,KY

Jane GALLAWAY-205
(Spouse of no. 1)

6 George EATON-446
B:
P:
M: -- 189
P:
D:
P:

12 John EATON-554
B:
P:
M: -- 327
P:
D:
P:

24
B:
M:
D:

25
B:
D:

13
B:
P:
D:
P:

26
B:
M:
D:

27
B:
D:

3 Sarah EATON-214
B: Abt 1776
P:
D:
P:

7 Catherine TUSA-447
B: Abt 1760
P: Sweden
D:
P:

14
B:
P:
M:
P:
D:
P:

28
B:
M:
D:

29
B:
D:

15
B:
P:
D:
P:

30
B:
M:
D:

31
B:
D:

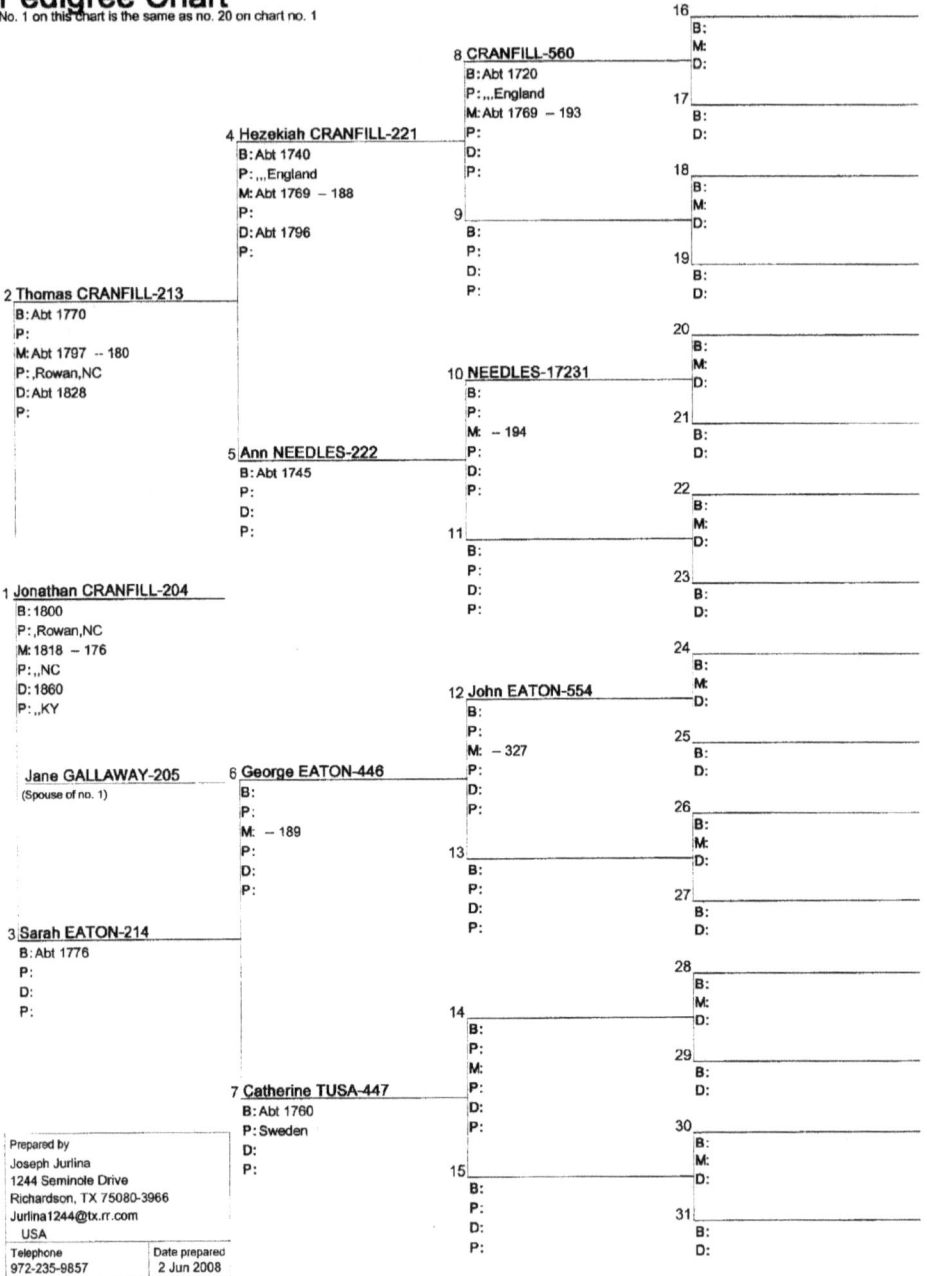

Prepared by
Joseph Jurlina
1244 Seminole Drive
Richardson, TX 75080-3966
Jurlina1244@tx.rr.com
USA
Telephone 972-235-9857
Date prepared 2 Jun 2008

Pedigree Chart

No. 1 on this chart is the same as no. 21 on chart no. 1

16
B:
M:
D:

8
B:
P:
M:
P:
D:
P:

17
B:
D:

4
B:
P:
M:
P:
D:
P:

18
B:
M:
D:

9
B:
P:
D:
P:

19
B:
D:

2 GALLOWAY-17227
B:
P:
M: -- 181
P:
D:
P:

20
B:
M:
D:

10
B:
P:
M:
P:
D:
P:

21
B:
D:

5
B:
P:
D:
P:

22
B:
M:
D:

11
B:
P:
D:
P:

23
B:
D:

1 Jane GALLAWAY-205
B: 15 Jan 1798
P: NC
M: 1818 -- 176
P: ,,NC
D: 1 Feb 1858
P: Calloway County,KY

24
B:
M:
D:

12
B:
P:
M:
P:
D:
P:

25
B:
D:

26
B:
M:
D:

Jonathan CRANFILL-204   6
(Spouse of no. 1)
B:
P:
M:
P:
D:
P:

13
B:
P:
D:
P:

27
B:
D:

3
B:
P:
D:
P:

28
B:
M:
D:

14
B:
P:
M:
P:
D:
P:

29
B:
D:

7
B:
P:
D:
P:

30
B:
M:
D:

15
B:
P:
D:
P:

31
B:
D:

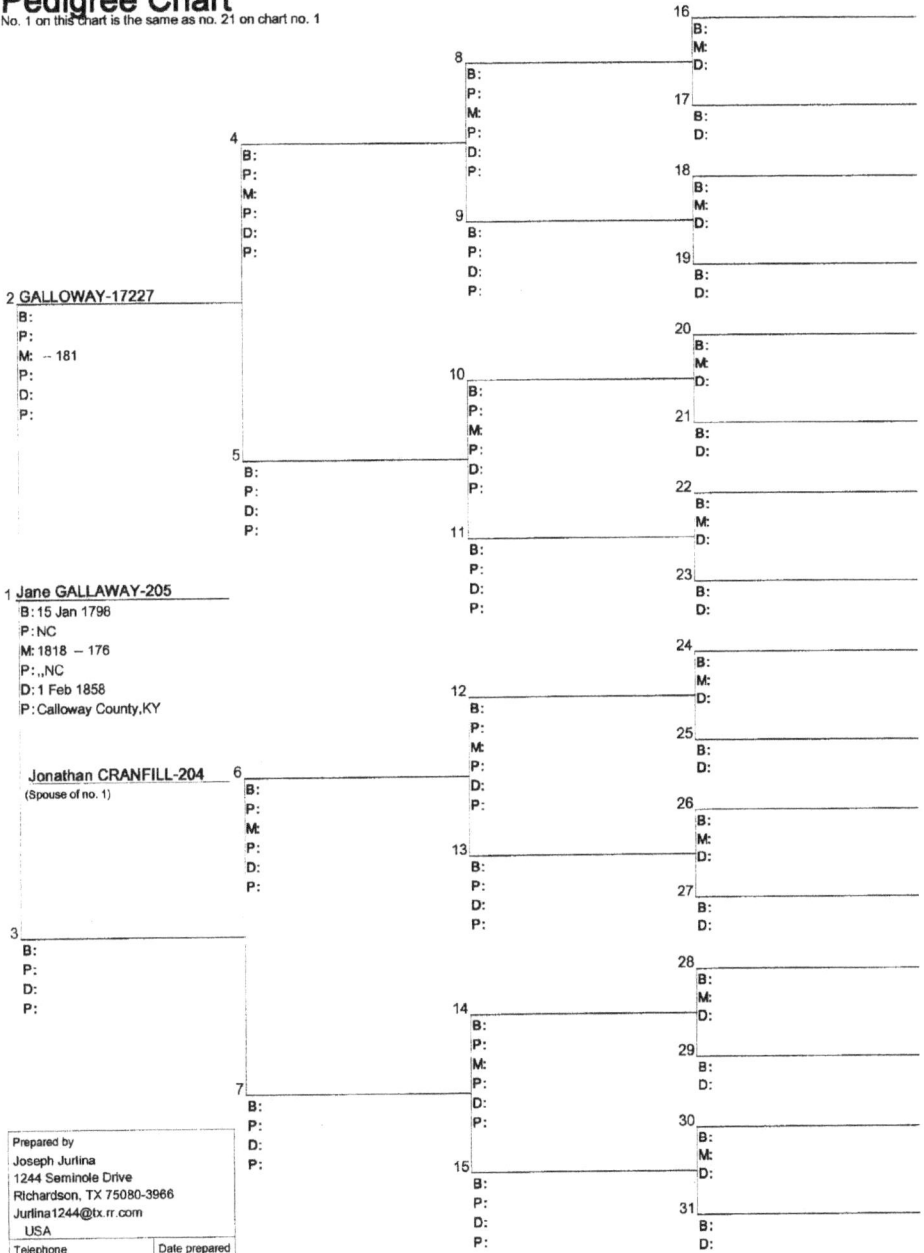

Prepared by
Joseph Jurlina
1244 Seminole Drive
Richardson, TX 75080-3966
Jurlina1244@tx.rr.com
USA

Telephone	Date prepared
972-235-9857	2 Jun 2008

Pedigree Chart

No. 1 on this chart is the same as no. 22 on chart no. 1

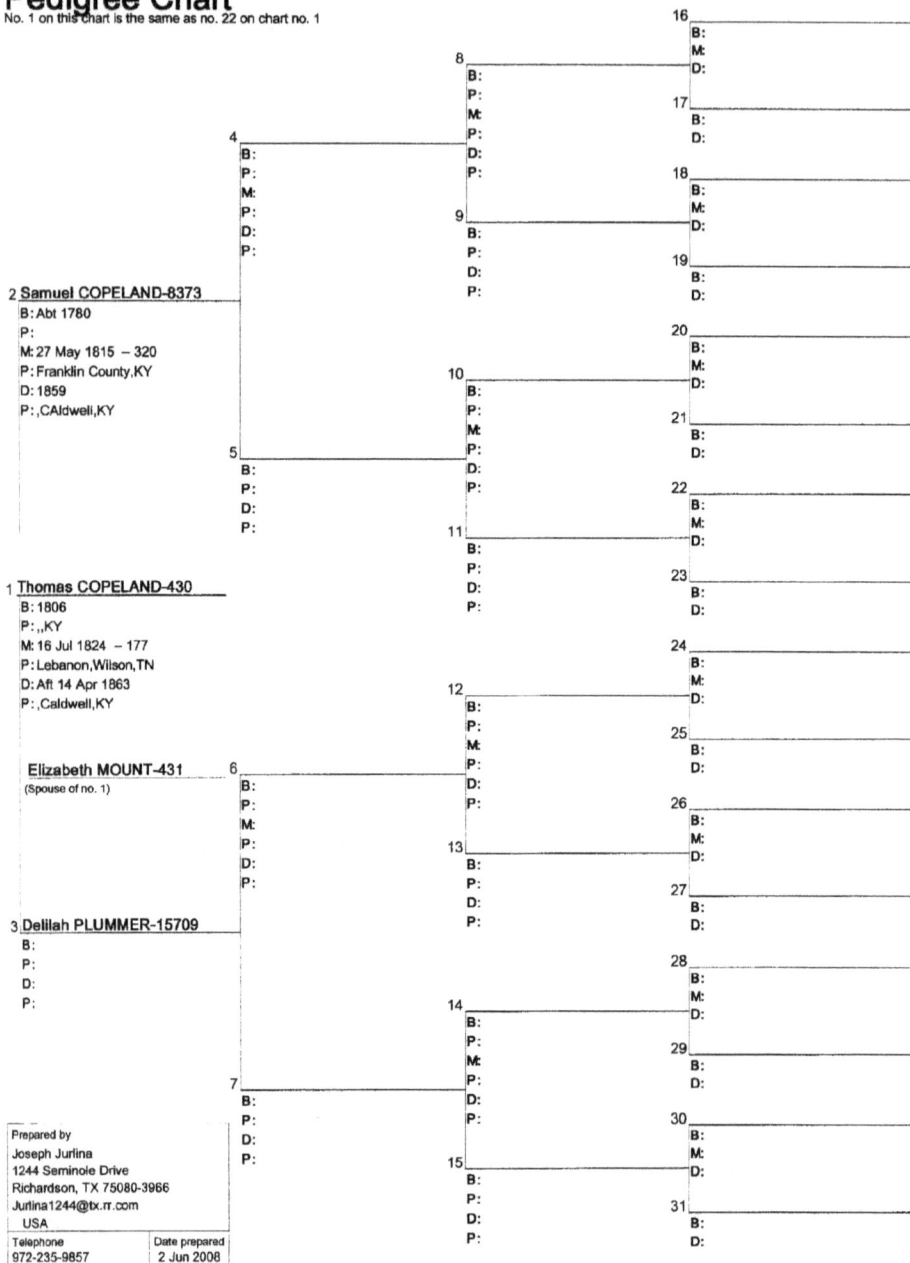

```
                                                                    16
                                                                      B:
                                                                      M:
                                                8                     D:
                                                 B:
                                                 P:              17
                                                 M:                   B:
                        4                        P:                   D:
                         B:                      D:
                         P:                      P:              18
                         M:                                           B:
                         P:                                           M:
                         D:                     9                     D:
                         P:                      B:
                                                 P:              19
                                                 D:                   B:
  2 Samuel COPELAND-8373                         P:                   D:
    B: Abt 1780
    P:                                                           20
    M: 27 May 1815  – 320                                             B:
    P: Franklin County,KY                                             M:
    D: 1859                                     10                    D:
    P: ,CAldweli,KY                              B:
                                                 P:              21
                        5                        M:                   B:
                         B:                      P:                   D:
                         P:                      D:
                         D:                      P:              22
                         P:                                           B:
                                                                      M:
                                                11                    D:
                                                 B:
                                                 P:              23
  1 Thomas COPELAND-430                          D:                   B:
    B: 1806                                      P:                   D:
    P: ,,KY
    M: 16 Jul 1824  – 177                                        24
    P: Lebanon,Wilson,TN                                             B:
    D: Aft 14 Apr 1863                                               M:
    P: ,Caldwell,KY                             12                   D:
                                                 B:
                                                 P:              25
                                                 M:                  B:
    Elizabeth MOUNT-431       6                  P:                  D:
    (Spouse of no. 1)          B:                D:
                               P:                P:              26
                               M:                                   B:
                               P:                                   M:
                               D:               13                  D:
                               P:                B:
                                                 P:              27
                                                 D:                 B:
  3 Delilah PLUMMER-15709                        P:                 D:
    B:
    P:                                                           28
    D:                                                              B:
    P:                                                              M:
                                                14                  D:
                                                 B:
                                                 P:              29
                                                 M:                 B:
                               7                 P:                 D:
                                B:               D:
  Prepared by                   P:               P:             30
  Joseph Jurlina                D:                                  B:
  1244 Seminole Drive           P:                                 M:
  Richardson, TX 75080-3966                     15                 D:
  Jurlina1244@tx.rr.com                          B:
  USA                                            P:             31
  ────────────────────────                       D:                B:
  Telephone      Date prepared                   P:                D:
  972-235-9857   2 Jun 2008
```

66

Pedigree Chart

No. 1 on this chart is the same as no. 23 on chart no. 1

16 Matthias MOUNT-17189   15
B: 1706
M: — 6494
D: 7 Apr 1791

8 Matthias MOUNT-17187
B: 1734
P: NJ
M: — 6492
P:
D: 22 Dec 1807
P:

17 Annie DISBROW-17190
B: 1714
D: 23 Jun 1792

4 Matthias MOUNT-17177
B: Abt 1765
P: Vanderdoort, Polk, AR
M: — 3454
P:
D: 1834
P: NC

18
B:
M:
D:

9 Margaret -17188
B:
P:
D:
P:

19
B:
D:

2 Richard MOUNT Jr.-8371
B: 7 Dec 1786
P: NC
M: 16 Jan 1809 — 321
P: Wilson County, TN
D: 16 Dec 1870
P: Wilson County, TN

20
B:
M:
D:

10
B:
P:
M:
P:
D:
P:

21
B:
D:

5 Elizabeth CHAMBERS-17178
B:
P:
D: Bef 1820
P:

22
B:
M:
D:

11
B:
P:
D:
P:

23
B:
D:

1 Elizabeth MOUNT-431
B: 11 Dec 1809
P: Wilson County, TN
M: 16 Jul 1824 — 177
P: Lebanon, Wilson, TN
D: 1863
P:

24
B:
M:
D:

12
B:
P:
M:
P:
D:
P:

25
B:
D:

Thomas COPELAND-430   6
(Spouse of no. 1)
B:
P:
M:
P:
D:
P:

26
B:
M:
D:

13
B:
P:
D:
P:

27
B:
D:

3 Polly MARTIN-8372
B: Abt 1785
P:
D: 1831
P:

28
B:
M:
D:

14
B:
P:
M:
P:
D:
P:

29
B:
D:

7
B:
P:
D:
P:

30
B:
M:
D:

15
B:
P:
D:
P:

31
B:
D:

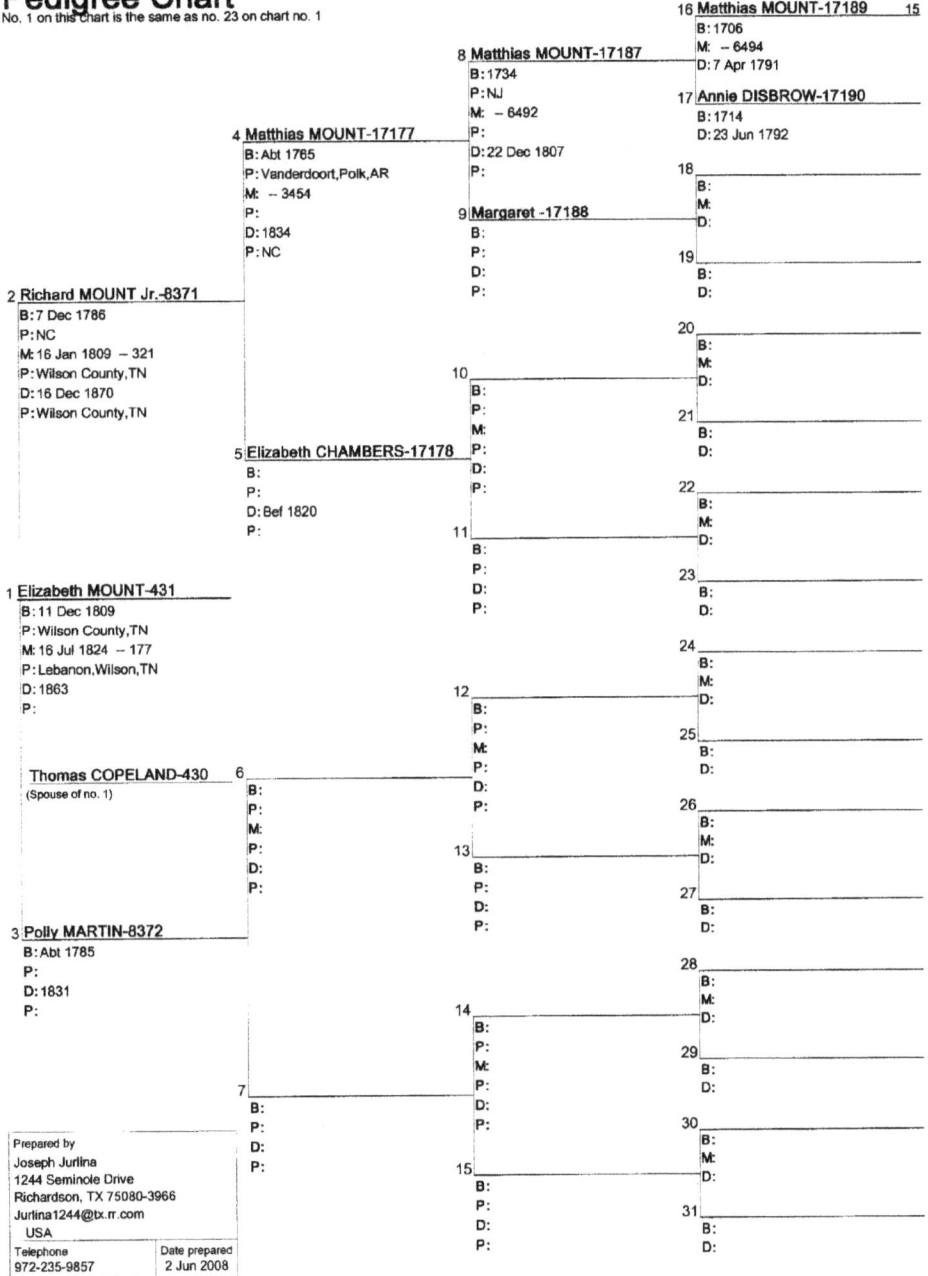

Prepared by
Joseph Jurlina
1244 Seminole Drive
Richardson, TX 75080-3966
Jurlina1244@tx.rr.com
USA

Telephone
972-235-9857

Date prepared
2 Jun 2008

67

Pedigree Chart

No. 1 on this chart is the same as no. 24 on chart no. 1

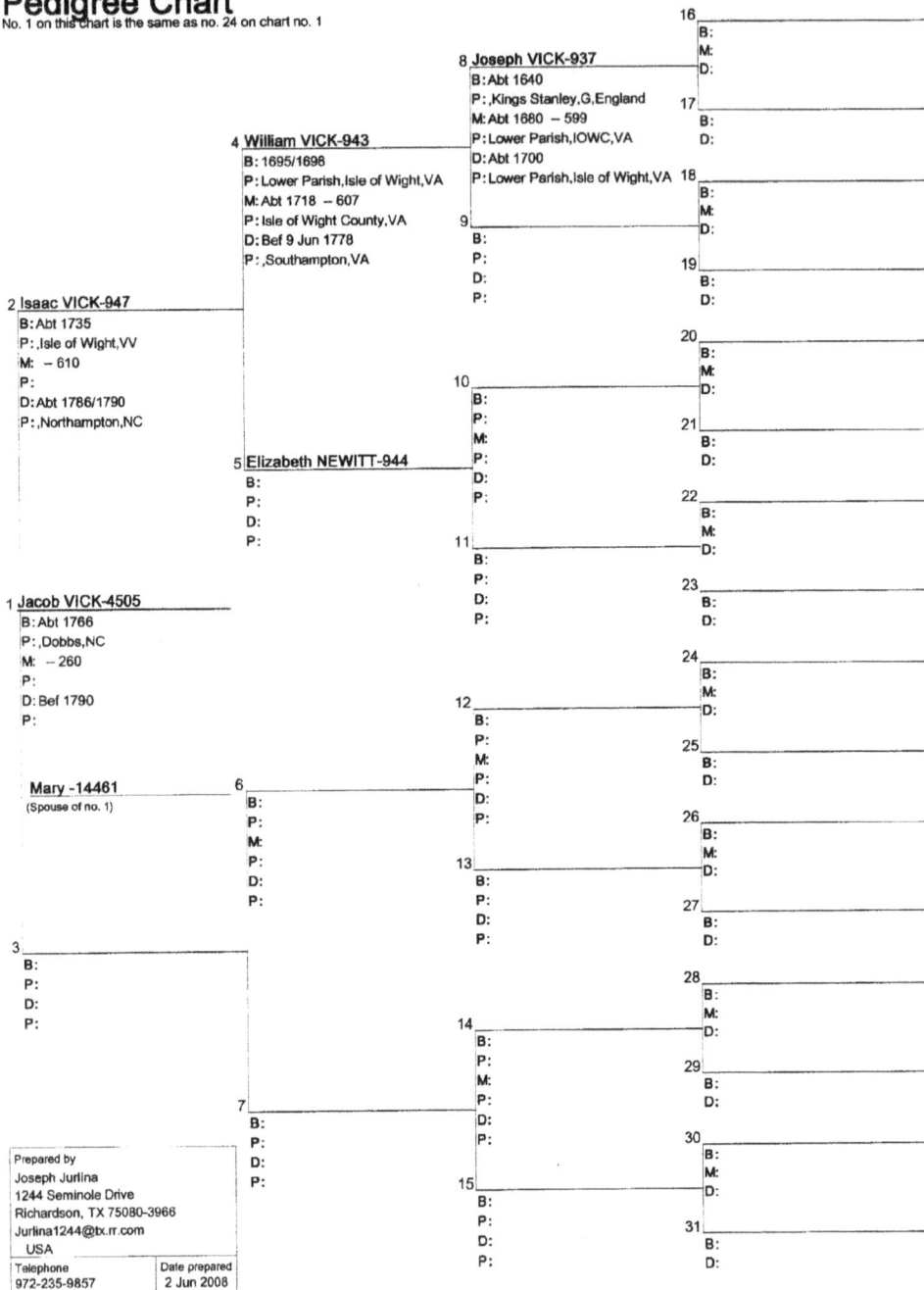

2 Isaac VICK-947
B: Abt 1735
P: ,Isle of Wight,VV
M: — 610
P:
D: Abt 1786/1790
P: ,Northampton,NC

4 William VICK-943
B: 1695/1698
P: Lower Parish,Isle of Wight,VA
M: Abt 1718 — 607
P: Isle of Wight County,VA
D: Bef 9 Jun 1778
P: ,Southampton,VA

8 Joseph VICK-937
B: Abt 1640
P: ,Kings Stanley,G,England
M: Abt 1680 — 599
P: Lower Parish,IOWC,VA
D: Abt 1700
P: Lower Parish,Isle of Wight,VA

5 Elizabeth NEWITT-944
B:
P:
D:
P:

1 Jacob VICK-4505
B: Abt 1766
P: ,Dobbs,NC
M: — 260
P:
D: Bef 1790
P:

Mary -14461
(Spouse of no. 1)

16 ___
B:
M:
D:

17 ___
B:
D:

18 ___
B:
M:
D:

19 ___
B:
D:

9 ___
B:
P:
D:
P:

20 ___
B:
M:
D:

21 ___
B:
D:

10 ___
B:
P:
M:
P:
D:
P:

22 ___
B:
M:
D:

23 ___
B:
D:

11 ___
B:
P:
D:
P:

24 ___
B:
M:
D:

25 ___
B:
D:

12 ___
B:
P:
M:
P:
D:
P:

26 ___
B:
M:
D:

27 ___
B:
D:

6 ___
B:
P:
M:
P:
D:
P:

13 ___
B:
P:
D:
P:

28 ___
B:
M:
D:

29 ___
B:
D:

3 ___
B:
P:
D:
P:

14 ___
B:
P:
M:
P:
D:
P:

30 ___
B:
M:
D:

31 ___
B:
D:

7 ___
B:
P:
D:
P:

15 ___
B:
P:
D:
P:

Prepared by
Joseph Jurlina
1244 Seminole Drive
Richardson, TX 75080-3966
Jurlina1244@tx.rr.com
USA

Telephone
972-235-9857

Date prepared
2 Jun 2008

68

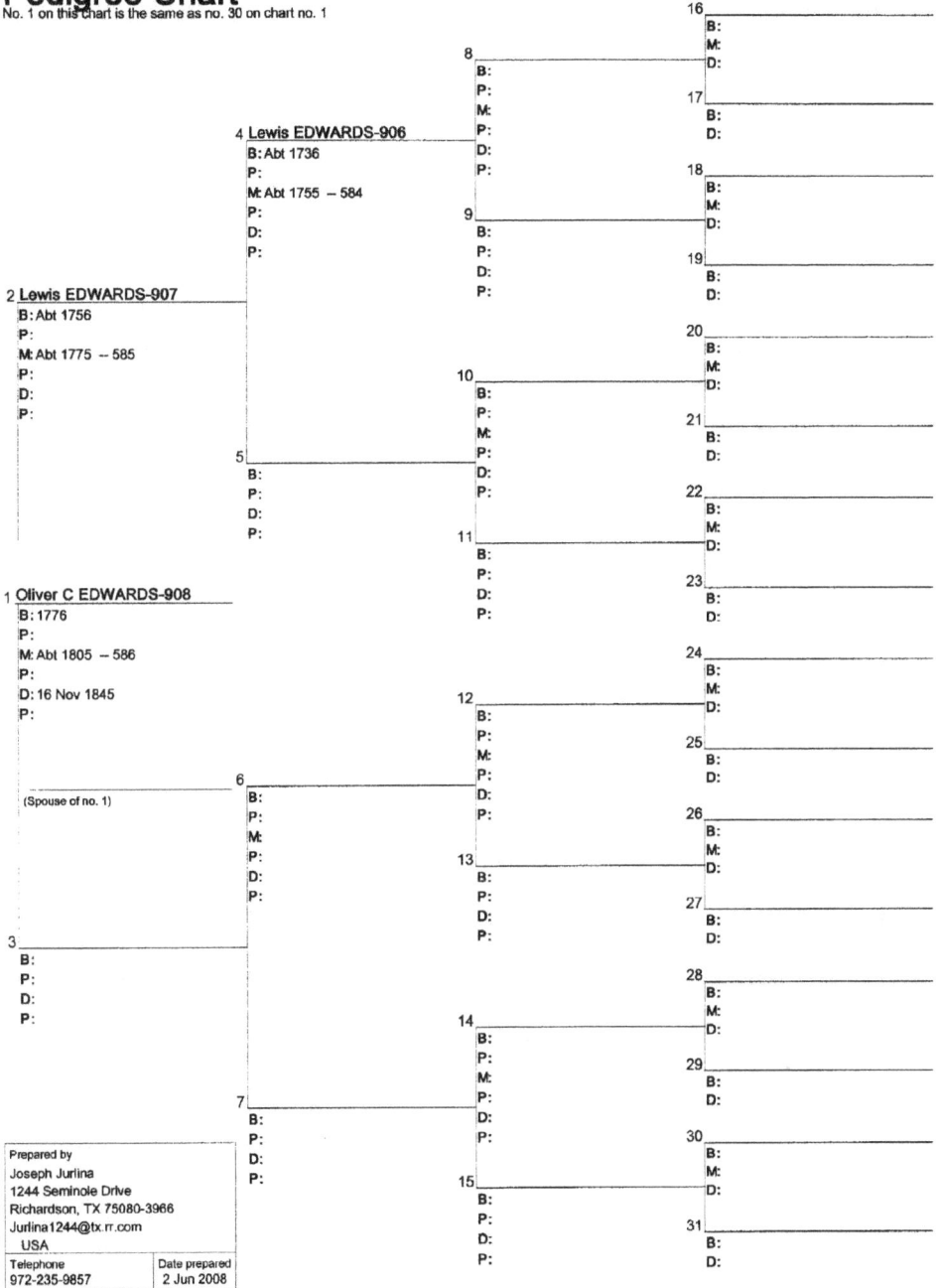

Pedigree Chart

No. 1 on this chart is the same as no. 30 on chart no. 1

16
B:
M:
D:

8
B:
P:
M:
P:
D:
P:

17
B:
D:

4 Lewis EDWARDS-906
B: Abt 1736
P:
M: Abt 1755 — 584
P:
D:
P:

18
B:
M:
D:

9
B:
P:
D:
P:

19
B:
D:

2 Lewis EDWARDS-907
B: Abt 1756
P:
M: Abt 1775 — 585
P:
D:
P:

20
B:
M:
D:

10
B:
P:
M:
P:
D:
P:

21
B:
D:

5
B:
P:
D:
P:

22
B:
M:
D:

11
B:
P:
D:
P:

23
B:
D:

1 Oliver C EDWARDS-908
B: 1776
P:
M: Abt 1805 — 586
P:
D: 16 Nov 1845
P:

24
B:
M:
D:

12
B:
P:
M:
P:
D:
P:

25
B:
D:

6
B:
P:
M:
P:
D:
P:

26
B:
M:
D:

(Spouse of no. 1)

13
B:
P:
D:
P:

27
B:
D:

3
B:
P:
D:
P:

28
B:
M:
D:

14
B:
P:
M:
P:
D:
P:

29
B:
D:

7
B:
P:
D:
P:

30
B:
M:
D:

15
B:
P:
D:
P:

31
B:
D:

Prepared by
Joseph Jurlina
1244 Seminole Drive
Richardson, TX 75080-3966
Jurlina1244@tx.rr.com
USA

| Telephone | Date prepared |
| 972-235-9857 | 2 Jun 2008 |

69

Pedigree Chart

No. 1 on this Chart is the same as no. 16 on chart no. 4

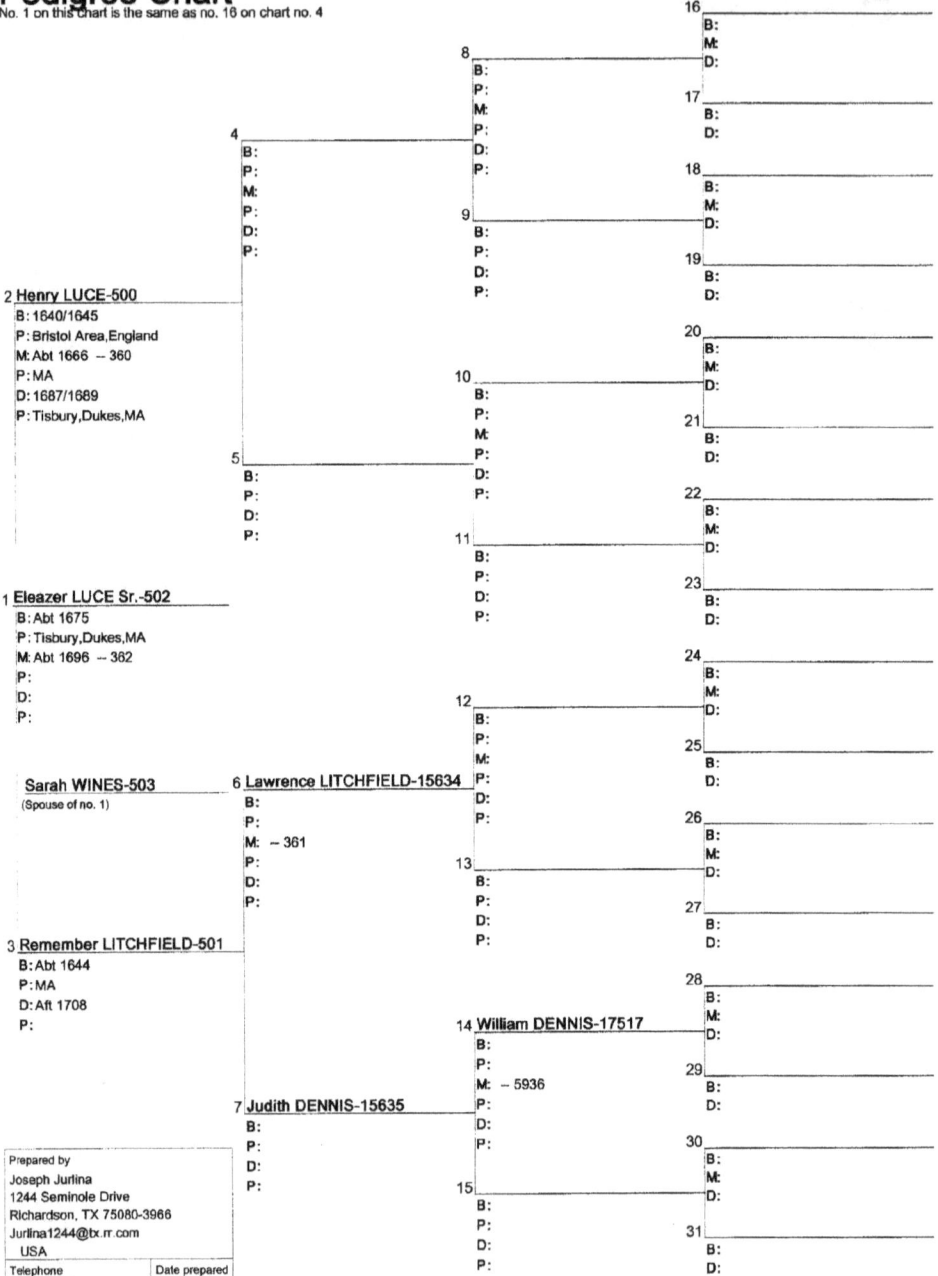

2 Henry LUCE-500
- B: 1640/1645
- P: Bristol Area,England
- M: Abt 1666 — 360
- P: MA
- D: 1687/1689
- P: Tisbury,Dukes,MA

1 Eleazer LUCE Sr.-502
- B: Abt 1675
- P: Tisbury,Dukes,MA
- M: Abt 1696 — 362
- P:
- D:
- P:

Sarah WINES-503
(Spouse of no. 1)

3 Remember LITCHFIELD-501
- B: Abt 1644
- P: MA
- D: Aft 1708
- P:

4
- B:
- P:
- M:
- P:
- D:
- P:

5
- B:
- P:
- D:
- P:

6 Lawrence LITCHFIELD-15634
- B:
- P:
- M: — 361
- P:
- D:
- P:

7 Judith DENNIS-15635
- B:
- P:
- D:
- P:

8
- B:
- P:
- M:
- P:
- D:
- P:

9
- B:
- P:
- D:
- P:

10
- B:
- P:
- M:
- P:
- D:
- P:

11
- B:
- P:
- D:
- P:

12
- B:
- P:
- M:
- P:
- D:
- P:

13
- B:
- P:
- D:
- P:

14 William DENNIS-17517
- B:
- P:
- M: — 5936
- P:
- D:
- P:

15
- B:
- P:
- D:
- P:

16
- B:
- M:
- D:

17
- B:
- D:

18
- B:
- M:
- D:

19
- B:
- D:

20
- B:
- M:
- D:

21
- B:
- D:

22
- B:
- M:
- D:

23
- B:
- D:

24
- B:
- M:
- D:

25
- B:
- D:

26
- B:
- M:
- D:

27
- B:
- D:

28
- B:
- M:
- D:

29
- B:
- D:

30
- B:
- M:
- D:

31
- B:
- D:

Prepared by
Joseph Jurlina
1244 Seminole Drive
Richardson, TX 75080-3966
Jurlina1244@tx.rr.com
USA

Telephone	Date prepared
972-235-9857	2 Jun 2008

Pedigree Chart

No. 1 on this chart is the same as no. 17 on chart no. 4

16 _____
B:
M:
D:

8 _____
B:
P:
M:
P:
D:
P:

17 _____
B:
D:

4 **Barnabas WINES SR.-17302**
B: Abt 1600
P: England
M: Abt 1620 – 367
P:
D: Abt 1676
P: Southold,Suffolk,NY

18 _____
B:
M:
D:

9 _____
B:
P:
D:
P:

19 _____
B:
D:

2 **Barnabas WINES Jr.-505**
B: Abt 1636
P: Watertown,Middlesex,MA
M: – 366
P:
D: Abt 1711
P:

20 _____
B:
M:
D:

10 **William EDDY-17304**
B:
P:
M: – 6540
P:
D:
P:

21 _____
B:
D:

5 **Anna EDDY-17303**
B: May 1603
P: Cranbrook,Kent,England
D:
P:

22 _____
B:
M:
D:

11 **Mary FOSTER-17305**
B:
P:
D:
P:

23 _____
B:
D:

1 **Sarah WINES-503**
B: 1668/1670
P: Southold,Suffolk,NY
M: Abt 1696 – 362
P:
D: 16 Apr 1733
P: Southold,Suffolk,NY

24 _____
B:
M:
D:

12 _____
B:
P:
M:
P:
D:
P:

25 _____
B:
D:

Eleazer LUCE Sr.-502
(Spouse of no. 1)

6 _____
B:
P:
M:
P:
D:
P:

26 _____
B:
M:
D:

13 _____
B:
P:
D:
P:

27 _____
B:
D:

3 **Mary MAPES-506**
B:
P:
D:
P:

28 _____
B:
M:
D:

14 _____
B:
P:
M:
P:
D:
P:

29 _____
B:
D:

7 _____
B:
P:
D:
P:

30 _____
B:
M:
D:

15 _____
B:
P:
D:
P:

31 _____
B:
D:

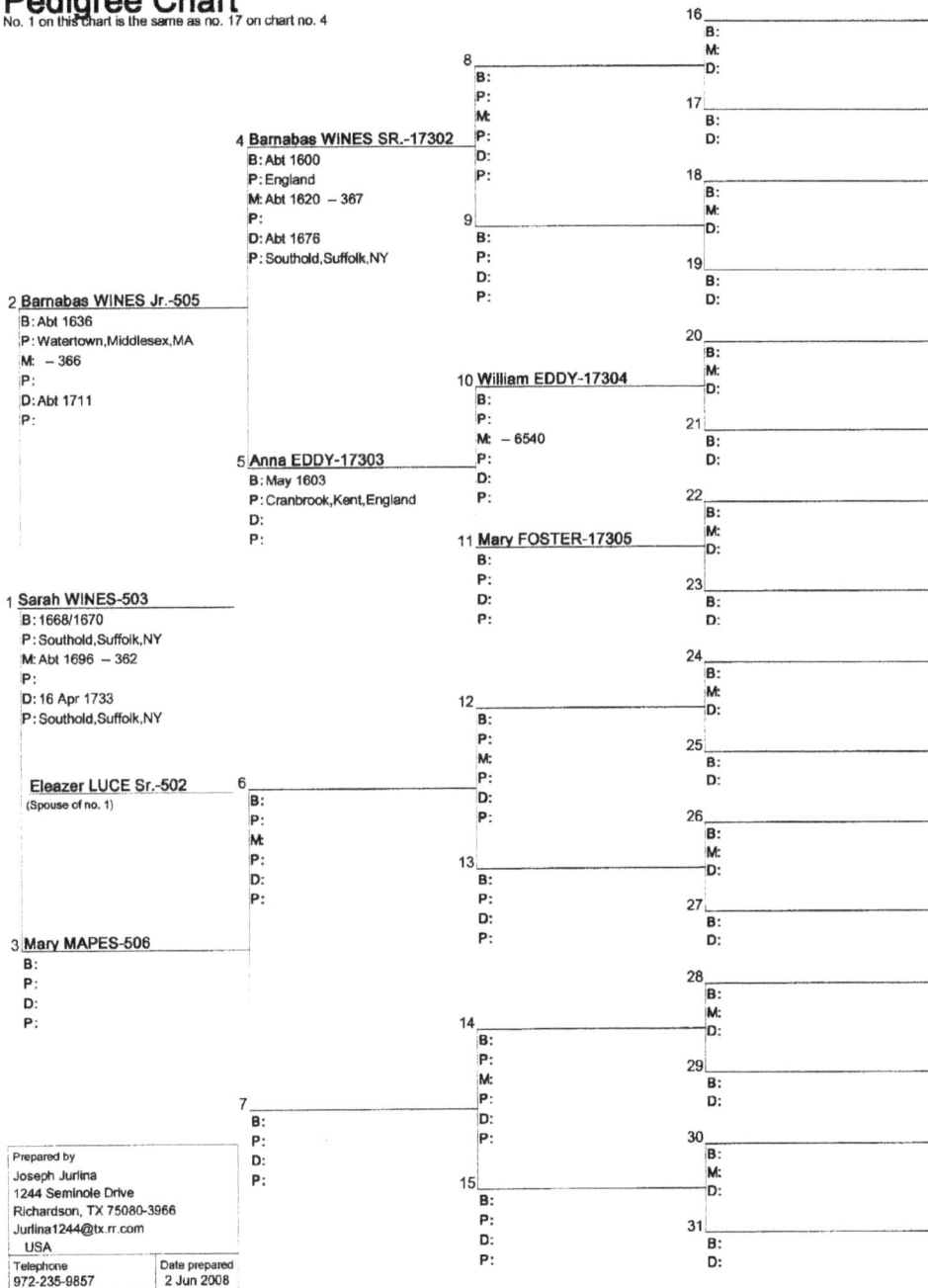

Prepared by
Joseph Jurlina
1244 Seminole Drive
Richardson, TX 75080-3966
Jurlina1244@tx.rr.com
USA

Telephone	Date prepared
972-235-9857	2 Jun 2008

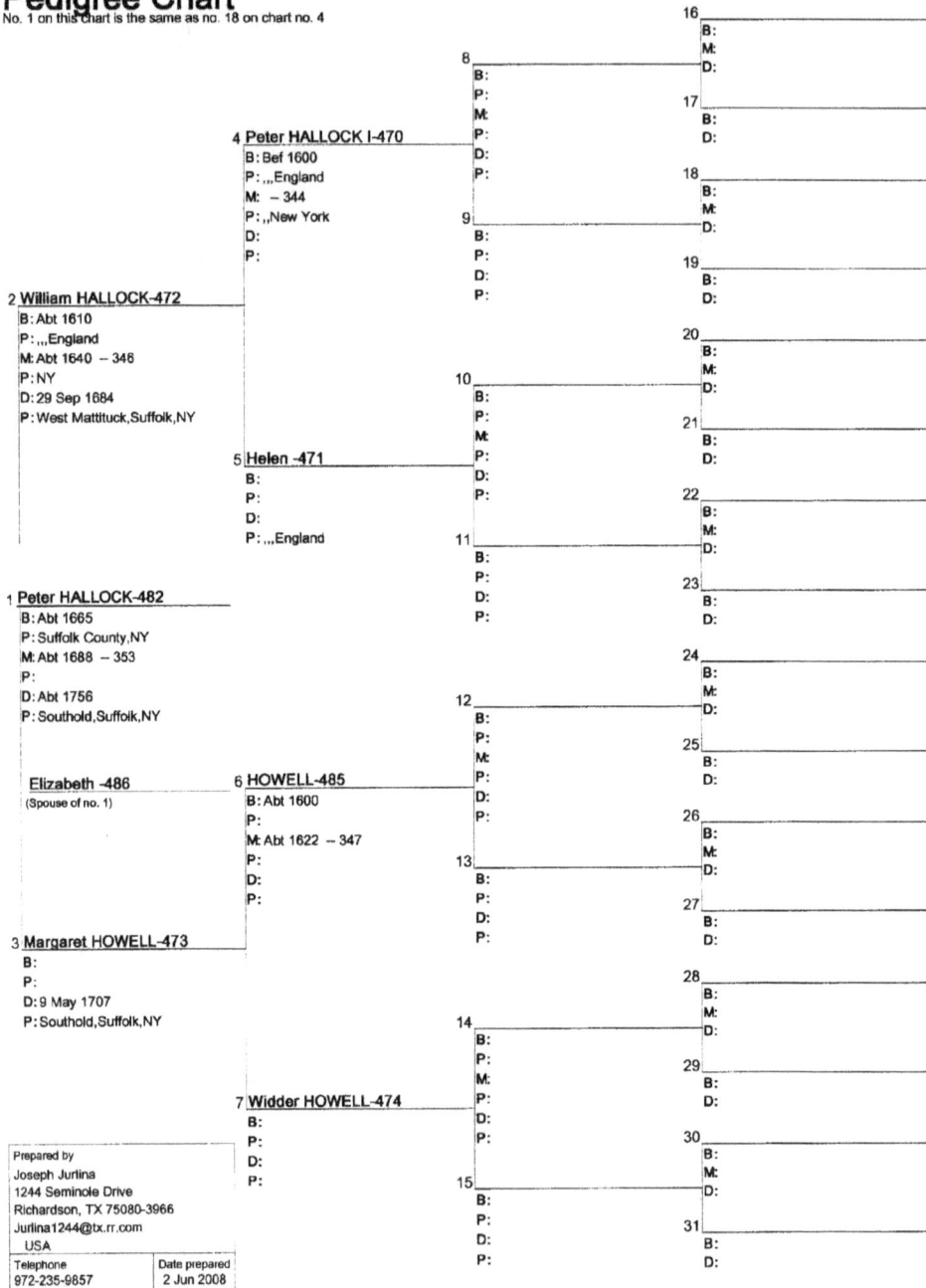

Pedigree Chart

2 William HALLOCK-472
B: Abt 1610
P: ,,,England
M: Abt 1640 — 346
P: NY
D: 29 Sep 1684
P: West Mattituck,Suffolk,NY

4 Peter HALLOCK I-470
B: Bef 1600
P: ,,,England
M: — 344
P: ,,New York
D:
P:

8
B:
P:
M:
P:
D:
P:

16
B:
M:
D:

17
B:
D:

9
B:
P:
D:
P:

18
B:
M:
D:

19
B:
D:

5 Helen -471
B:
P:
D:
P: ,,,England

10
B:
P:
M:
P:
D:
P:

20
B:
M:
D:

21
B:
D:

11
B:
P:
D:
P:

22
B:
M:
D:

23
B:
D:

1 Peter HALLOCK-482
B: Abt 1665
P: Suffolk County,NY
M: Abt 1688 — 353
P:
D: Abt 1756
P: Southold,Suffolk,NY

Elizabeth -486
(Spouse of no. 1)

6 HOWELL-485
B: Abt 1600
P:
M: Abt 1622 — 347
P:
D:
P:

12
B:
P:
M:
P:
D:
P:

24
B:
M:
D:

25
B:
D:

13
B:
P:
D:
P:

26
B:
M:
D:

27
B:
D:

3 Margaret HOWELL-473
B:
P:
D: 9 May 1707
P: Southold,Suffolk,NY

7 Widder HOWELL-474
B:
P:
D:
P:

14
B:
P:
M:
P:
D:
P:

28
B:
M:
D:

29
B:
D:

15
B:
P:
D:
P:

30
B:
M:
D:

31
B:
D:

Prepared by
Joseph Jurlina
1244 Seminole Drive
Richardson, TX 75080-3966
Jurlina1244@tx.rr.com
USA

Telephone	Date prepared
972-235-9857	2 Jun 2008

Pedigree Chart

No. 1 on this chart is the same as no. 20 on chart no. 4

1 William HALLOCK-483
B: Abt 1667
P:
M: Abt 1688 — 355
P:
D: Abt 1736
P:

Mary -17333   6
(Spouse of no. 1)

2 William HALLOCK-472
This person is the same as no. 2 on chart no. 13

3 Margaret HOWELL-473
This person is the same as no. 3 on chart no. 13

4 _____
B:
P:
M:
P:
D:
P:

5 _____
B:
P:
D:
P:

6 _____
B:
P:
M:
P:
D:
P:

7 _____
B:
P:
D:
P:

8 _____
B:
P:
M:
P:
D:
P:

9 _____
B:
P:
D:
P:

10 _____
B:
P:
M:
P:
D:
P:

11 _____
B:
P:
D:
P:

12 _____
B:
P:
M:
P:
D:
P:

13 _____
B:
P:
D:
P:

14 _____
B:
P:
M:
P:
D:
P:

15 _____
B:
P:
D:
P:

16 _____
B:
M:
D:

17 _____
B:
D:

18 _____
B:
M:
D:

19 _____
B:
D:

20 _____
B:
M:
D:

21 _____
B:
D:

22 _____
B:
M:
D:

23 _____
B:
D:

24 _____
B:
M:
D:

25 _____
B:
D:

26 _____
B:
M:
D:

27 _____
B:
D:

28 _____
B:
M:
D:

29 _____
B:
D:

30 _____
B:
M:
D:

31 _____
B:
D:

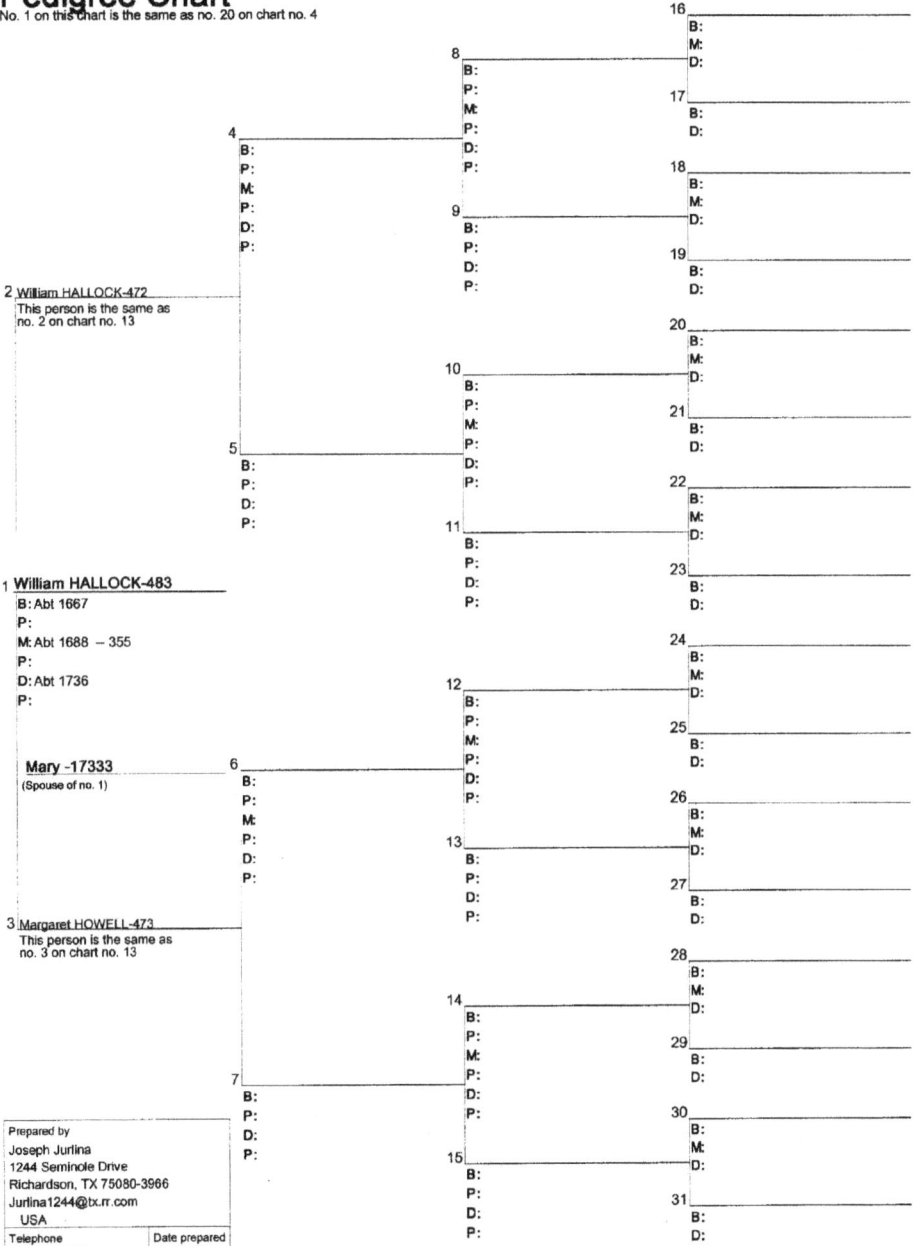

Prepared by
Joseph Jurlina
1244 Seminole Drive
Richardson, TX 75080-3966
Jurlina1244@tx.rr.com
USA

Telephone	Date prepared
972-235-9857	2 Jun 2008

73

Pedigree Chart

No. 1 on this chart is the same as no. 16 on chart no. 8

```
                                                              16
                                                                  B:
                                          8 George MOUNT-17220     M:
                                            B: Abt 1635             D:
                                            P: England          17
                                            M: -- 6507             B:
                        4 Matthias MOUNT-17215  P: RI              D:
                          B: Abt 1668         D:
                          P: NJ               P:                18
                          M: -- 6502                              B:
                          P:                                      M:
                          D: 1695           9 Katherine BORDEN?-17221  D:
                          P:                  B:
                                              P:                19
    2 Matthias MOUNT-17206                     D:                  B:
      B:                                       P:                  D:
      P:
      M: -- 6495                                               20
      P:                                                          B:
      D:                          10                              M:
      P:                            B:                            D:
                                    P:                         21
                        5 Mary WALL-17216   M:                    B:
                          B: 1663          P:                     D:
                          P:               D:
                          D: 1700          P:                  22
                          P:                                      B:
                                        11                        M:
                                          B:                      D:
                                          P:                   23
  1 Matthias MOUNT-17189                   D:                     B:
    B: 1706                                P:                     D:
    P: NJ
    M: -- 6494                                                 24
    P:                                                            B:
    D: 7 Apr 1791                        12                       M:
    P:                                     B:                      D:
                                          P:                   25
                                          M:                      B:
       Annie DISBROW-17190      6          P:                     D:
       (Spouse of no. 1)          B:       D:
                                  P:       P:                  26
                                  M:                              B:
                                  P:                              M:
                                  D:     13                       D:
                                  P:       B:
                                           P:                  27
    3 Ann NESBIT-17207                     D:                     B:
      B:                                   P:                     D:
      P:
      D:                                                       28
      P:                                                          B:
                                        14                        M:
                                          B:                      D:
                                          P:                   29
                                          M:                      B:
                                7          P:                     D:
                                  B:       D:
                                  P:       P:                  30
                                  D:                              B:
                                  P:     15                       M:
                                           B:                     D:
                                           P:                  31
                                           D:                     B:
                                           P:                     D:
```

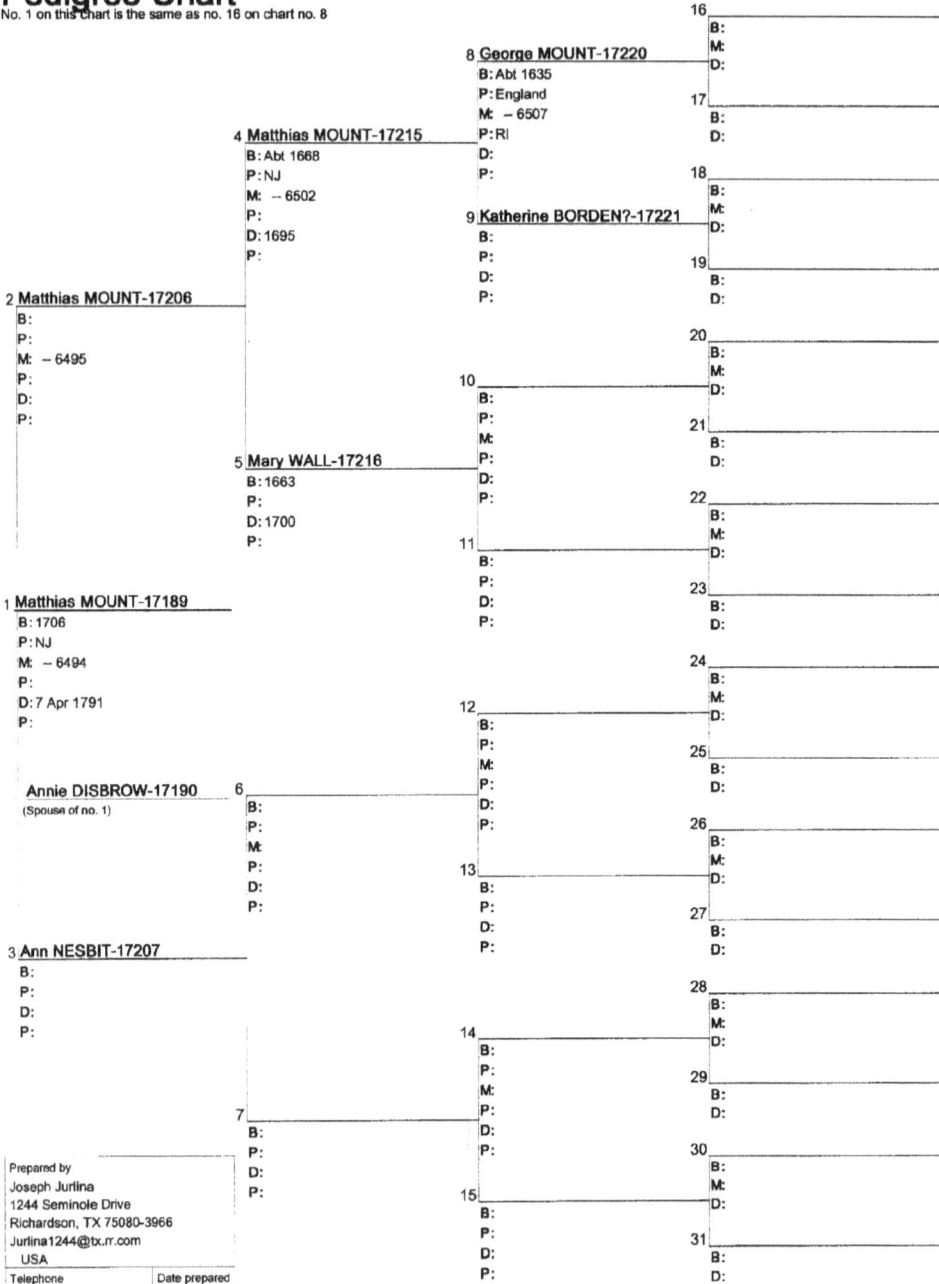

Prepared by
Joseph Jurlina
1244 Seminole Drive
Richardson, TX 75080-3966
Jurlina1244@tx.rr.com
USA

Telephone
972-235-9857

Date prepared
2 Jun 2008

74

Pedigree Chart
Alphabetical Index

RIN	Name	Born /Chr	Died /Bur	Found on Chart	Position
486	, Elizabeth			4	19
471	, Helen			13	5
17188	, Margaret			8	9
17333	, Mary			4	21
14461	, Mary	Abt 1764		1	25
17221	BORDEN?, Katherine			15	9
17178	CHAMBERS, Elizabeth		Bef 1820	8	5
8373	COPELAND, Samuel	Abt 1780	1859	7	2
200	COPELAND, Sarah Torksey	13 Apr 1834	15 May 1904	1	11
430	COPELAND, Thomas	1806	Aft 14 Apr 1863	1	22
524	CORCORAN, Mary		1826	4	7
560	CRANFILL,	Abt 1720		5	8
221	CRANFILL, Hezekiah	Abt 1740	Abt 1796	5	4
199	CRANFILL, Isom W.	11 Dec 1831	15 Mar 1902	1	10
100	CRANFILL, Jane	30 Dec 1854	14 Mar 1941	1	5
204	CRANFILL, Jonathan	1800	1860	1	20
213	CRANFILL, Thomas	Abt 1770	Abt 1828	5	2
15635	DENNIS, Judith			11	7
17517	DENNIS, William			11	14
17190	DISBROW, Annie	1714	23 Jun 1792	8	17
6331	DUFF, Mary			3	3
446	EATON, George			5	6
554	EATON, John			5	12
214	EATON, Sarah	Abt 1776		5	3
17303	EDDY, Anna	May 1603		12	5
17304	EDDY, William			12	10
909	EDWARDS, Alcey Ann	Abt 1816	14 Sep 1862	1	15
906	EDWARDS, Lewis	Abt 1736		10	4
907	EDWARDS, Lewis	Abt 1756		10	2
908	EDWARDS, Oliver Cromwell	1776	16 Nov 1845	1	30
17305	FOSTER, Mary			12	11
205	GALLAWAY, Jane	15 Jan 1798	1 Feb 1858	1	21
17227	GALLOWAY,			6	2
2	GRABLE, Billie John	28 Sep 1924		1	1
36	GRABLE, John Francis	4 Mar 1880	30 Mar 1952	1	2
7750	GRABLE, Philip	Abt 1740		2	2
240	GRABLE, Samuel A.	Abt 1780	Abt 1838	1	16
99	GRABLE, Virgil Lee	10 Oct 1850	1927	1	4
228	GRABLE, Wilson Lee	25 Sep 1827	6 Dec 1883	1	8
487	HALLOCK, Abiah	Cal 1702	13 Dec 1765	4	9
520	HALLOCK, Mehitable	27 Oct 1742	9/10 Sep 1825	4	5
482	HALLOCK, Peter	Abt 1665	Abt 1756	4	18
470	HALLOCK, Peter I	Bef 1600		13	4
472	HALLOCK, William	Abt 1610	29 Sep 1684	13	2
483	HALLOCK, William	Abt 1667	Abt 1736	4	20
518	HALLOCK, Zebulon	Abt 1694	9 Mar 1785	4	10
485	HOWELL,	Abt 1600		13	6
473	HOWELL, Margaret		9 May 1707	13	3
474	HOWELL, Widder			13	7
1	JURLINA, Joseph	19 Sep 1924		1	Spouse
15634	LITCHFIELD, Lawrence			11	6
501	LITCHFIELD, Remember	Abt 1644	Aft 1708	11	3
259	LOPP, Mary Elizabeth	22 Sep 1854	10 Jun 1938	1	7
914	LOPP, William M.	Abt 1820		1	14
507	LUCE, Abner	15/18 Mar 1738	30 Sep 1818	4	4
504	LUCE, Eleazer Jr.	Abt 1700	15 May 1759	4	8
502	LUCE, Eleazer Sr.	Abt 1675		4	16
500	LUCE, Henry	1640/1645	1687/1689	11	2
452	LUCE, Nancy Elizabeth	11 Jan 1811	25 May 1845	1	19
467	LUCE, William	16 Jul 1767	22 Jul 1843	4	2
506	MAPES, Mary			12	3
8372	MARTIN, Polly	Abt 1785	1831	8	3
241	MILLHOUSE, Mary	Abt 1783	1838	1	17
431	MOUNT, Elizabeth	11 Dec 1809	1863	1	23
17220	MOUNT, George	Abt 1635		15	8
17177	MOUNT, Matthias	Abt 1765	1834	8	4

Pedigree Chart

Alphabetical Index

RIN	Name	Born /Chr	Died /Bur	Found on Chart	Position
17187	MOUNT, Matthias	1734	22 Dec 1807	8	8
17189	MOUNT, Matthias	1706	7 Apr 1791	8	16
17206	MOUNT, Matthias			15	2
17215	MOUNT, Matthias	Abt 1668	1695	15	4
8371	MOUNT, Richard Jr.	7 Dec 1786	16 Dec 1870	8	2
17231	NEEDLES,			5	10
222	NEEDLES, Ann	Abt 1745		5	5
17207	NESBIT, Ann			15	3
944	NEWITT, Elizabeth			9	5
468	NEWMAN, Nancy Ann	17 Oct 1771	8 Sep 1836	4	3
523	NEWMAN, Thomas	1746	1820	4	6
15709	PLUMMER, Delilah			7	3
17129	REEVES, Jonathan			4	22
519	REEVES, Martha	1701	13 Feb 1780	4	11
229	SIMMONS, Mary Anne	18 Jun 1830	10 Jun 1908	1	9
451	SIMMONS, Richard H. Sr.	1804	21 May 1866	1	18
535	SIMMONS, William	Bef 1740	Abt 1816	3	2
315	SKINNER, Elizabeth	Abt 1817		1	13
447	TUSA, Catherine	Abt 1760		5	7
947	VICK, Isaac	Abt 1735	Abt 1786/1790	9	2
314	VICK, Isaiah	13 Nov 1785	13 Mar 1873	1	12
4505	VICK, Jacob	Abt 1766	Bef 1790	1	24
937	VICK, Joseph	Abt 1640	Abt 1700	9	8
258	VICK, Nathan Monroe	15 Dec 1850	6 Dec 1918	1	6
943	VICK, William	1695/1698	Bef 9 Jun 1778	9	4
35	VICK, Willie Laura	6 Oct 1886	2 Oct 1960	1	3
17216	WALL, Mary	1663	1700	15	5
17302	WINES, Barnabas SR.	Abt 1600	Abt 1676	12	4
505	WINES, Barnabas Jr.	Abt 1636	Abt 1711	12	2
503	WINES, Sarah	1668/1670	16 Apr 1733	4	17

Appendix B:
Genealogical Records

Form No. 7 A

TEXAS DEPARTMENT OF HEALTH
BUREAU OF VITAL STATISTICS

Certificate No. __not known__

Place of Birth ___Whitt___ Date of Birth ___Sep 1, 1909___

Full Name of Child ___Not named___ *(Mabel Louise)*

Sex ___F___ Twin or Otherwise ___Not given___

Color or Race ___White___ Legitimate ___Yes___
Parents--Native

Name of Father ___Jno. Grable (and wife)___ *(Eddie Laura)*

Maiden Name of Mother ___Hicks___

Residence ___Whitt___

Physician or Person Reporting Birth:

L. A. Lindsey	Whitt
Name	Address

File Date ___October 1, 1909___

THE STATE OF TEXAS)
COUNTY OF PARKER) I, ___Carrie Reed___ , Clerk of the County Court of

Parker County, Texas do hereby certify that the above and foregoing birth certificate of

___Un named___ is a true and correct copy of the same

as shown of record in Vol. __2__, Page __213__ of the Birth Records of Parker County,

Texas.

Witness my hand and seal of office this __30th__ day of __September__ A.D., 19 __88__.

Carrie Reed
COUNTY CLERK, PARKER COUNTY, TEXAS

(SEAL)

By ___Donna Brooks___ Deputy.

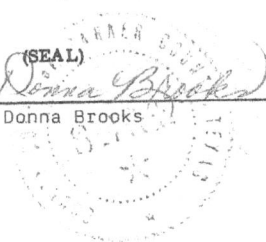

77

BIRTH RECORD

U-516-A

1. PLACE OF BIRTH	TEXAS DEPARTMENT OF HEALTH	FILE No.
STATE OF TEXAS	BUREAU OF VITAL STATISTICS	
County of Parker	STANDARD CERTIFICATE OF BIRTH	Register No.

City or Precinct No. Whitt, Texas

Give Street and Number or Name of Institution

2. Full Name of Child John Aaron Grable

Residence of the Mother, Street and No. _____ City _____ County _____ State

3. Sex	FOR PLURAL BIRTHS ONLY:	6. Legitimate?	7. Date of Birth
Male	4. Twin, Triplet, Other	5. Number, In Order of Birth	Yes	December 5th, 1904 , 194

FATHER	MOTHER
8. Full Name John Francis Grable	14. Full Maiden Name Willie Laura Vick
Social Security Number	Social Security Number
9. Postoffice Address Whitt, Texas	15. Postoffice Address Whitt, Texas
10. Color or Race White 11. Age at Last Birthday 25 (Years)	16. Color or Race White 17. Age at Last Birthday 16 (Years)
12. Birthplace (State or Country) Texas	18. Birthplace (State or Country) Louisiana
Occupation 13A. Trade, Profession Kind of Work Done Groceryman	Occupation 19A. Trade or Profession Kind of Work Done Housewife
13B. Industry Business in Which Engaged Grocery Store	19B. Industry Business in Which Engaged Home
20. Number of Children Born to This Mother including This Birth 1	21. Number of Children Born to This Mother and Now Living 1
Signature of Informant Mrs. J. F. Grable	Address of Informant Throckmorton , Texas

22. Medical Attendance

I HEREBY CERTIFY That I attended the birth of this Child Born Alive Stillborn At _____ 11 A _____ M. on the above date.

And the Prophylactic used to prevent Ophthalmia Neonatorum was _____

Dec. 5 ___ 1904 J. D. Pickens _____ M. D. Midwife _____ Postoffice Address _____ , Texas

info. from birth record at Parker Co. Annex was recorded original birth date as "Willie Dee" rather than John Aaron -

23. File Number	File Date	Signature of Local Register
	, 194	

CORRECTION AFFIDAVIT

STATE OF TEXAS }
COUNTY OF _____

Before me on this day appeared _____ known to me to be the person whose name is signed to the above certificate, who on oath deposes and says that the facts stated in the foregoing certificate are true and correct to the best of his her knowledge and belief, and that this certificate is filed for the purpose of correcting the original record of birth of _____

(Name appearing on original certificate)

Signature _____

Sworn to and subscribed before me, this _____ day of _____ , 194

Notary Public in and for _____ County, Texas

AFFIDAVIT A

STATE OF OHIO
DEPARTMENT OF HEALTH
DIVISION OF VITAL STATISTICS
CERTIFICATE OF BIRTH

County of _____ **CUYAHOGA**

Township of _____
or
Village of _____
or
City of _____ **CLEVELAND**

Registration District No. _____

File No. _____

No. _1157 E 63_ St.

Primary Registration District No. _____

Registered No. _**16121**_

_23_ Ward.

FULL NAME OF CHILD _Joseph Jurlina_

(If child is not yet named, make supplemental report, as directed)

Sex of Child _Male_	Twin, triplet or other? (To be answered only in event of plural births)	Number in order of birth	Legitimate _Yes_	Date of birth _Oct._ _19_, 192_4_ (Month) (Day) (Year)	

FATHER

FULL NAME _Thomas Jurlina_

RESIDENCE Including P. O. Address _1157 E 63 St_

COLOR OR RACE _W_   AGE AT LAST BIRTHDAY _17_ (Years)

BIRTHPLACE _Jugo-Slavia_

OCCUPATION AND INDUSTRY _Laborer_

MOTHER

FULL MAIDEN NAME _Mary Telban_

RESIDENCE Including P. O. Address _1167 E 63_

COLOR OR RACE _W_   AGE AT LAST BIRTHDAY _20_ (Years)

BIRTHPLACE _U.S._

OCCUPATION AND INDUSTRY _Housewife_

NUMBER OF CHILDREN BORN AND LIVING

Number of children born alive to this mother, including this child (if born alive) _1_

Number of children of this mother living, including this child (if born alive) _1_

Was Prophylactic against Ophthalmia Neonatorum used? _Yes_
(On request, Prophylactic and literature furnished free by OHIO DEPARTMENT OF HEALTH)

CERTIFICATE OF ATTENDING PHYSICIAN OR MIDWIFE*

I hereby certify that I attended the birth of this child born to _Mary Jurlina_ and that the
(Mother's Name)
child was _alive_ at _4_ a. M., on the date above stated.
(Born alive or Stillborn)

* When there was no attending physician or midwife, then the father, householder, etc., should make this return. A stillborn child is one that neither breathes nor shows other evidence of life after birth.

Given name added from a supplemental report

_____, 192__

(Signature) _Maryane Puc_

Date _____ 192__ Address _7085 E 64 St._

I HEREBY CERTIFY THAT
R. P. Ochsner, M.D.
FILE IN THE DEPT.
HEALTH CLEVELAND, OHIO

Filed _Oct 1_

TEXAS DEPARTMENT OF HEALTH
BUREAU OF VITAL STATISTICS
CERTIFICATE OF BIRTH

1. PLACE OF BIRTH
STATE OF TEXAS

COUNTY OF __Young__

CITY OR PRECINCT NO. __Olney__

GIVE STREET AND NUMBER OR NAME OF INSTITUTION

2. FULL NAME OF CHILD __BILLIE JOHN GRABLE__

3. SEX	FOR PLURAL BIRTHS ONLY:		6. LEGITIMATE?	7. DATE OF BIRTH
Female	4. TWIN, TRIPLET, OTHER	5. NUMBER, IN ORDER OF BIRTH	Yes	September 28, 1924

FATHER	MOTHER
8. FULL NAME John F. Grable	14. FULL MAIDEN NAME Willie L. Vick
9. RESIDENCE AT TIME OF THIS BIRTH Throckmorton, Texas	15. RESIDENCE AT TIME OF THIS BIRTH Throckmorton, Texas
10. COLOR OR RACE White 11. AGE AT TIME OF THIS BIRTH 40 YEARS	16. COLOR OR RACE White 17. AGE AT TIME OF THIS BIRTH 34 YEARS
12. BIRTHPLACE (STATE OR COUNTRY) Texas	18. BIRTHPLACE (STATE OR COUNTRY) La.
13A. TRADE, PROFESSION OR KIND OF WORK DONE Farming	19A. TRADE, PROFESSION OR KIND OF WORK DONE Housewife
13B. INDUSTRY OR BUSINESS IN WHICH ENGAGED	19B. INDUSTRY OR BUSINESS IN WHICH ENGAGED
27. NUMBER OF CHILDREN BORN TO THIS MOTHER, INCLUDING THIS BIRTH 3	21. NUMBER OF CHILDREN BORN TO THIS MOTHER, AND NOW LIVING 3

I HEREBY CERTIFY TO THE BIRTH OF THIS CHILD WHO WAS BORN ALIVE AT __3 P.__ M. ON THE DATE STATED ABOVE.

22. SIGNATURE __H. C. McKinney__   ADDRESS __Olney, Texas__

MEDICAL ATTENDANT'S AFFIDAVIT*

STATE OF TEXAS

COUNTY OF __Young__

BEFORE ME ON THIS DAY APPEARED __Dr. H. C. McKinney__
(Name of Physician)

KNOWN TO ME TO BE THE PERSON WHO SIGNED THE FOREGOING CERTIFICATE OF BIRTH, WHO ON OATH DEPOSES AND SAYS THAT HE/SHE WAS THE MEDICAL ATTEND-

ANT AT THE BIRTH OF __Billie John Grable__, AND THAT THE FACTS
(Name Appearing on Certificate)

STATED IN THE CERTIFICATE ATTACHED HERETO ARE TRUE AND CORRECT TO THE BEST OF HIS/HER KNOWLEDGE AND BELIEF.

SIGNATURE OF PHYSICIAN __H. C. McKinney__

SWORN TO AND SUBSCRIBED BEFORE ME, THIS __17__ DAY OF __October__, 194__4__

(SEAL) __Grace Rodgers__

NOTARY PUBLIC IN AND FOR __Young__ COUNTY, TEXAS

AFFIDAVIT A

STATE OF TEXAS

COUNTY OF

BEFORE ME ON THIS DAY APPEARED

KNOWN TO ME TO BE THE PERSON WHO SIGNED THE CERTIFICATE ATTACHED HERETO, WHO ON OATH DEPOSES AND SAYS THAT THE FACTS STATED IN THE FORE-

GOING BIRTH CERTIFICATE OF _____ ARE TRUE AND CORRECT TO THE BEST OF HIS/HER
(Name Appearing on Certificate)

KNOWLEDGE AND BELIEF, AND THAT HE/SHE WAS ACQUAINTED WITH THE FACTS AT THE TIME OF THE EVENT.

SIGNATURE

SWORN TO AND SUBSCRIBED BEFORE ME, THIS _____ DAY OF _____, 194__

NOTARY PUBLIC IN AND FOR _____ COUNTY, TEXAS

(SEAL)

AFFIDAVIT B

STATE OF TEXAS

COUNTY OF

BEFORE ME ON THIS DAY APPEARED

KNOWN TO ME TO BE THE PERSON WHO SIGNED THIS AFFIDAVIT, WHO ON OATH DEPOSES AND SAYS THAT THE FACTS STATED IN THE FOREGOING BIRTH CERTIFICATE

OF _____ ARE TRUE AND CORRECT TO THE BEST OF HIS/HER
(Name Appearing on Certificate)

KNOWLEDGE AND BELIEF, AND THAT HE/SHE IS ACQUAINTED WITH THE FACTS AND THAT HE/SHE IS NOT RELATED TO THE INDIVIDUAL BY BLOOD OR MARRIAGE.

SIGNATURE

SWORN TO AND SUBSCRIBED BEFORE ME, THIS _____ DAY OF _____, 194__

NOTARY PUBLIC IN AND FOR _____ COUNTY, TEXAS

(SEAL)

STATE OF TEXAS

COUNTY OF __Young__

THE BIRTH CERTIFICATE OF __Billie John Grable__

ATTACHED HERETO, WAS SUBMITTED TO THIS COURT, AS PROVIDED FOR IN H. B. NO. 614, 46TH LEG., R. S. 1939.

IT IS THE ORDER OF THIS COURT THAT THIS RECORD BE ACCEPTED / BE NOT ACCEPTED BY THE STATE REGISTRAR FOR FILING IN THE STATE BUREAU OF VITAL STATISTICS.

SIGNATURE __Raymon Thompson__ COUNTY JUDGE

(handwritten right margin: Vol. 8, page 386 - Young Co, Tx)

TEXAS DEPARTMENT OF HEALTH
BUREAU OF VITAL STATISTICS

FILE NO. 154494-46

NAME CAROL ANN JURLINA

DATE OF BIRTH 11-25-46   SEX   FEMALE

PLACE OF BIRTH TRAVIS COUNTY TEXAS

FATHER
JOSEPH JOHN JURLINA

MOTHER
BILLIE JOHN GRABLE

DATE FILED 12-09-46   DATE ISSUED   10-07-88

This is a true certification of name and birth facts
as recorded in this office. Issued under authority of
Rule 54a, Article 4477, Revised Civil Statutes of Texas.

J. L. Howze

J. L. HOWZE
STATE REGISTRAR

CERTIFICATION OF BIRTH

TEXAS DEPARTMENT OF HEALTH
BUREAU OF VITAL STATISTICS

FILE NO. 186108-52

NAME MICHAEL KENNETH JURLINA

DATE OF BIRTH 10-20-52   SEX   MALE

PLACE OF BIRTH DALLAS COUNTY TEXAS

FATHER
JOSEPH JOHN JURLINA

MOTHER
BILLIE JOHN GRABLE

DATE FILED 12-09-52   DATE ISSUED   10-07-88

This is a true certification of name and birth facts
as recorded in this office. Issued under authority of
Rule 54a, Article 4477, Revised Civil Statutes of Texas.

J. L. Howze

J. L. HOWZE
STATE REGISTRAR

CERTIFICATION OF BIRTH

Marriage License

STATE OF TEXAS
COUNTY OF THROCKMORTON

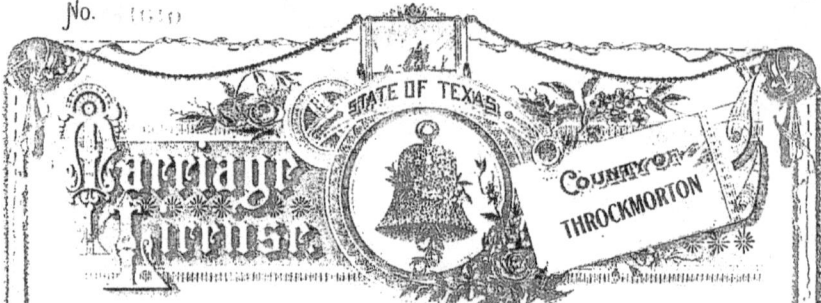

To any Regularly Licensed or Ordained Minister of the Gospel, Jewish Rabbi, Judge of the District or County Court, or any Justice of the Peace

IN THE STATE OF TEXAS—GREETING:

You are hereby Authorized to Solemnize the

RITES OF MATRIMONY

BETWEEN

Mr. Joseph John Jenlina and Miss Billie John Grable and make due return to the Clerk of the County Court of said County within sixty days thereafter certifying your action under this License

Witness my official signature and seal of office at office in Throckmorton the 12 day of May 1945.

Calvin Whitaker

Deputy Clerk of County Court Throckmorton County

I Joe Z Tower hereby certify that on the 12th day of May 1945 I joined in Marriage Joseph John Jenlina and Billie John Grable the parties above named

Witness my hand this 12th day of May 1945

Joe Z Tower Pastor First Methodist Church Wichita Falls Texas

I Calvin Whitaker Clerk County Court Throckmorton County Texas hereby certify that the above is the original Marriage License issued to the above named parties and with the return thereon was duly recorded in my **office in book** 3 page 231 of Marriage License Record of Throckmorton County on the 15 day May 1945

Witness my hand and seal of office this the 15 day of May 1945

Calvin Whitaker

Deputy County Clerk Throckmorton County

THE STATE OF TEXAS,
PARKER COUNTY.

No. 621.

To any Judge of the County or District Court, Regularly Licensed or Ordained Minister of the Gospel, Jewish Rabbi, or Justice of the Peace in and for said County of Parker, GREETING:

YOU ARE HEREBY AUTHORIZED TO SOLEMNIZE THE RITES OF MATRIMONY BETWEEN

Mr. J. F. Grable and Miss Millie Vick

and make due return to the Clerk of the County Court of said County within sixty days thereafter, certifying your action under this License.

WITNESS my official signature and seal of office, at office in Weatherford, this ......19...... day of ...Nov...... A. D. 1902.

J. E. Hodges
Clerk of the County Court, Parker County.

By O. L. McFall ....Deputy.

I, L. B. Loxley, hereby certify that on the 19th day of Nov. A. D. 1902 I united in Marriage Mr. J. F. Grable and Miss Willie Vick the parties above named.

WITNESS my hand this 19th day of November A. D. 1902.

L. B. Loxley
Minister officiating

Returned and filed for record the 8th day of Dec. 1902, and recorded the 13 day of April 1903.

J. E. Hodges ....County Clerk.

By ....Deputy.

RECORD OF MARRIAGE LICENSES

The Dorsey Company, Stationers, Dallas, Tex. 1913

THE STATE OF TEXAS
County of _Throckmorton_

To Any Regularly Licensed or Ordained Minister of the Gospel, Jewish Rabbi, Judge of the District or County Court, or any Justice of the Peace in the State of Texas—GREETING:

YOU ARE HEREBY AUTHORIZED TO SOLEMNIZE THE RITES OF MATRIMONY

Between Mr. _Thomas E. Boyd_ and Miss _Louise Grable_ and make due return to the Clerk of the County Court of said County within sixty days thereafter, certifying your action under this License.

WITNESS MY OFFICIAL SIGNATURE AND SEAL OF OFFICE, At office in _Throckmorton_ the _8_ day of _March,_ A.D. 19_30_.

Kate Beaty

[L.S.] _Seal_.

Clerk of the County Court _Throckmorton_ Co., Texas.

By _____ Deputy.

I, _C. B. Yeargan_, certify that on the _8th_ day of _March_ A.D. 19_30_ I united in Marriage Mr. _Thomas E. Boyd_ and Miss _Louise Grable_ the parties above named.

WITNESS MY HAND This _8th_ day of _March_ A.D. 19_30_.

C. B. Yeargan

Presbyterian Minister

RETURNED AND FILED FOR RECORD The _10_ day of _March_ A.D. 19_30_ and recorded the _9_ day of _April_ A.D. 19_30_

Kate Beaty County Clerk.

By _____ Deputy.

RECORD OF MARRIAGE LICENSES

The Dorsey Company, Stationers, Dallas, Tex. 1913

THE STATE OF TEXAS
County of _Throckmorton_

To Any Regularly Licensed or Ordained Minister of the Gospel, Jewish Rabbi, Judge of the District or County Court, or any Justice of the Peace in the State of Texas—GREETING:

YOU ARE HEREBY AUTHORIZED TO SOLEMNIZE THE RITES OF MATRIMONY

Between Mr. _John A. Grable_ and Miss _Beulah Lou Lee_ and make due return to the Clerk of the County Court of said County within sixty days thereafter, certifying your action under this License.

WITNESS MY OFFICIAL SIGNATURE AND SEAL OF OFFICE, At office in _Throckmorton_ the _2_ day of _June_ A.D. 19_30_.

Kate Beaty

[L.S.] _Seal_

Clerk of the County Court _Throckmorton_ Co., Texas.

By _____ Deputy.

I, _Rev. B. C. Taylor_, certify that on the _5_ day of _June_ A.D. 19_30_ I united in Marriage _John A. Grable_ and Miss _Beulah Lou Lee_ the parties above named.

WITNESS MY HAND This _5_ day of _June_ A.D. 19_30_.

B. C. Taylor

RETURNED AND FILED FOR RECORD The _7_ day of _June_ A.D. 19_30_ and recorded the _10_ day of _June_ A.D. 19_30_

Kate Beaty County Clerk.

By _____ Deputy.

June 5, 1930

MISS BEAULAH LOW LEE AND MR. JOHN A. GRABLE
ARE MARRIED AT M.E. CHURCH

The wedding of Miss Beaulah Low Lee to Mr. John A. Grable was solemnized Thursday evening, June 5th, at the First Methodist Church of Throckmorton, Rev. Byron C. Taylor of Mer Rouge, LA pronouncing the ceremony.

The church was beautifully decorated with ferns and baskets of Gladiolas.

Prior to the ceremony Miss Ouida Clemonts of Abilene sang "I Love You Truly" and "At Dawning". The "Wedding March" from Lohengren was rendered as a processional by Mr. Alfred Alexander and Miss Camilla Marrs of Abilene. During the wedding service they played "To a Wild Rose" by Macdowell and Mendelsohn's "Wedding March" as a recessional.

Miss Ruth Lee, sister of the bride, maid of honor, wore beige chiffon with lace trimmings. The other attendants were: Miss Bessie Watson, of Corsicana, wearing orchid satin with accessories to match, Mrs. Tomas E. Boyd of Throckmorton, wearing orchid taffeta and accessories to match, Miss Opal Johnson of Abilene, wearing peach satin with lace trimmings, and Miss Pauline Braddock, of Graham, wearing peach taffeta with tulle trimmings.

Mr. Douglas C. Newman of Bryson was best man. The ushers were: Edgar L. Lee and Bascom Story, of Graford.

The following were flower girls: Misses Mary Nell Bailey of Graford and Betsy Carpenter of Throckmorton, wearing pale green organdie and Billie John Grable and Precious Parrott of Throckmorton, wearing pink and orchid organdie.

The train bearers were: Misses Carmendene Hitchcock and Billie Jean De Lane wearing light green georgette.

Little John Lee Brown in a suit of white linen carried the platinum band on a white tulle pillow.

The fair bride was a pleasing picture in a wedding frock of white satin and trimmings of tulle. Her veil of tulle and lace was held in place by a crown of orange blossoms and she carried a shower of bride's roses and valley lilies. The bride entered on the arm of her grandfather, Mr. R. H. Pate.

The bride is the daughter of Mr. & Mrs. R. P. Lee of Throckmorton. She is a graduate of McMurray College, Abilene.

The groom is the only son of Mr. & Mrs. J. F. Grable of Throckmorton. He is a graduate of Hardin Simmons University of Abilene and has taught in the Abilene city schools this past two years. A reception for the bridal party and relatives followed the ceremony, the affair being held in the home of the bride. The handsome bridal cake was served with brick ice cream.

After the reception the bride slipped away and changed into a green crepe suit with hat and accessories to match.

Mr. & Mrs. Grable left for a tour to Galveston and will make their future home in Throckmorton.

Out-of-town guests included: Mr. & Mrs. R. H. Howell, Graham; Rev. & Mrs. Byron C. Taylor, Mer Rouge, La; Mr. & Mrs. F. C. Hughes, Dallas; Mr. & Mrs. J. P. Bailey and family, Graford; Mrs. M. L. Story and sons, Graford; Mrs. B. P. Story, Ft. Worth; Mr. & Mrs. S. F. Lee and family, Graford; Mr. R. H. Pate, Graford; Mrs. V. A. Sikes, Graford; Mesdames W. L. Barrett and Kenneth Sparks, Mineral Wells; Ms. Eda Watson, Corsicana; Mrs. W. E. Braddock, Graham; Mrs. J. C. Tipps and son, Charles, Eldorado, Ark; Mrs. N. M. Vick, Sweetwater; Misses Edessa Kuykendall, Camilla Marrs, and Lillian Meadows, and Mr. Burney Blaine, Abilene.

TEXAS DEPARTMENT OF HEALTH
BUREAU OF VITAL STATISTICS
STANDARD CERTIFICATE OF DEATH

1 PLACE OF DEATH
STATE OF TEXAS

COUNTY OF *Jack*   Registrar's No. *8*

CITY OR PRECINCT NO. *Perrin*   No. *2*   Street

If in an institution, give name of institution instead of Street and No.

Length of residence in city where death occurred *5* yrs. ___ mos. ___ days. How long in U. S. if foreign born? ___ yrs. ___ mos. ___ days.

2 FULL NAME OF DECEASED *Mrs. Mary Vick*

RESIDENCE OF THE DECEASED No. ___ St. ___ City *Perrin* State *Texas*

PERSONAL AND STATISTICAL PARTICULARS

3. SEX *Female*   4. COLOR OR RACE *White*   5. Single, Married, Widowed, Divorced (Write the word) *Widowed*

5a. If married, widowed, or divorced HUSBAND of (or) WIFE of *Nathan Vick*

6. DATE OF BIRTH (month, day, and year) *September 22, 1854*

7. AGE *83* Years *8* Months *18* Days

8. Trade, profession, or particular kind of work done, as spinner, sawyer, bookkeeper, etc.

9. Industry or business in which work was done, as silk mill, saw mill, bank, etc.

10. Date deceased last worked at this occupation (month and year)

11. Total time (years) spent in this occupation

12. BIRTHPLACE (City or Town) (State or Country) *Tarrant Co Texas*

FATHER 13. NAME *Bill Lopp*
14. BIRTHPLACE (City or Town) (State or Country) *Germany*

MOTHER 15. MAIDEN NAME *alcey ann Edwards*
16. BIRTHPLACE (City or Town) (State or Country) *Missouri*

17. INFORMANT *Mrs J. J. King*
(Address) *1010 E. Hubbard Mineral Wells Texas*

18. BURIAL *White Texas*
REMOVAL Place ___ Date *June 11 1938*

19. UNDERTAKER *R. H. Butham*
(Address) *Mineral Wells Texas*

20. SIGNATURE AND FILE DATE OF LOCAL REGISTRAR
June 24 1938 (File Date) *(Signature)*

MEDICAL PARTICULARS

20. DATE OF DEATH (month, day, and year) *198__*

21. I HEREBY CERTIFY, That I attended deceased from *May 30 1938* to *June 10 1938*
I last saw ___ alive on *June 10 198__*; death is said to have occurred on the date stated above, at *9:30* ___ m.

The principal cause of death and related causes of importance as follows:

Paralysis   Date of Onset

Other contributory causes of importance: *senility*

(8) Serial ___ Number of Discharge ___
or ADJUSTED SERVICE CERTIFICATE

What test confirmed diagnosis? ___ Was there an autopsy? ___

22. If death was due to external causes (violence) fill in also the following:

Accident, suicide, or homicide? ___   Date of injury ___ 193__

Where did injury occur? ___
(Specify city or town, county, and State)

Specify whether injury occurred in industry, in home, or in public place

Manner of injury ___

Nature of injury ___

24. Was disease or injury in any way related to occupation of deceased? ___

If so, specify ___

(Signed) *O. E. Stringer*
(Address) *Perrin Texas*

STATE death certificate Number
28702

John Grable Dies At Throckmorton

THROCKMORTON, Oct. 29 (Special)—John A. Grable, 47, former Merkel automobile dealer and stock farmer here for the past eight years, died Wednesday night in a Throckmorton hospital following an illness of four and one-half months.

Born in Whitt, Tex., Dec. 5, 1904, Grable moved to Throckmorton with his parents at the age of 12. It was here that he met and married Beulah Low Lee June 5, 1930. Shortly after the marriage, the couple moved to Merkel, where Grable was associated in an automobile agency.

Eight years ago the family moved back to Throckmorton, where Grable had since engaged in stock farming. He was a member of the Methodist Church and the Masonic Lodge.

Surviving are his widow, two sons, John R. and Jerry Grable, his mother, Mrs. J. F. Grable, all of Throckmorton; two sisters, Mrs. Joe Jurline, Dallas, and Mrs. Thomas Boyd, Throckmorton.

Funeral services will be held Thursday at 3 p.m. in the First Methodist Church, with Rev. R. S. Watkins, pastor, and Rev. Tilden Armstrong, pastor of the Floydada church, officiating.

Interment will be in the Throckmorton cemetery—under direction of the Merriman Funeral Home.

PRESS NOTES

Mrs. Willie Grable Dies; Throck Rites

THROCKMORTON (RNS) — Mrs. Willie Laura Grable, 72, a local resident since 1917, died Sunday in Dallas. She had been in poor health for about a year and had been in Dallas two months.

She married John F. Grable in Whitt in 1902. They came to Throckmorton from Parker County. Her husband died several years ago. He was a farmer.

Funeral was held at 4 p.m. Monday at the First Methodist Church here with the pastor, the Rev. Carl McMasters, officiating. Burial was in Throckmorton Cemetery with Merriman Funeral Home in charge.

Survivors include two daughters, Mrs. Thomas Boyd of Throckmorton and Mrs. Joe Jurlina of Dallas; six grandchildren and three great-grandchildren.

Mrs. Willie Grable

Mrs. Willie Grable, 72, whose daughter Mrs. Joe Jurlina lives at 2727 Wilbur, died Sunday in a Dallas hospital following a long illness.

Mrs. Grable had been a resident of Throckmorton, Throckmorton County, for 45 years, but came to Dallas six months ago to enter a hospital.

Born in Louisiana, Mrs. Grable moved with her parents to Whitt in Parker County at an early age and lived there for many years. She was a member of the First Methodist Church in Throckmorton.

Survivors include another daughter, Mrs. Thomas Boyd of Throckmorton and six grandchildren and three great grandchildren.

Funeral services will be held at 3 p.m. Monday at the First Methodist Church in Thorckmorton with burial in Throckmorton Cemetery.

John F. Grable Is Laid to Rest Sun.

John Francis Grable, 72-year-old retired farmer and rancher, died at 1:30 a. m. here Sunday in the Throckmorton County Memorial Hospital.

Funeral services were held at 4 p. m. the same day from the First Methodist Church with Rev. Clem Lewis, pastor, and Rev. K. M. Kerrick, pastor of the First Baptist Church, officiating. Burial was in the Throckmorton Cemetary under the direction of Merriman Funeral Home.

Grable, born March 4, 1880, in Parker County, had lived here for the past 35 years. He was a member of the Methodist Church here for more than 25 years.

Survivors include his wife of Throckmorton; a son, John A. Grable of Throckmorton; two daughters, Mrs. Thomas Boyd of Throckmorton and Mrs. Joseph Jurlina of Cleveland, Ohio; two sisters, seven brothers, and five grandchildren and one great grandchild.

Pallbearers were Floyd Beach, Henry Johnson, Johnnie Keeter, W. S. Nelson, Roy Fant, and Dick Stout of Throckmorton, and Ira Lauderdale and Robert Calvin of Graford.

J. F. Grable Dies In Throckmorton

THROCKMORTON, Tex., March 30 (Special)—John Francis Grable, 72-year-old retired farmer and rancher, died at 1:30 a.m. here today in Throckmorton County Memorial Hospital.

Funeral services were held at 4 p.m. today from the First Methodist Church with Rev. Clem Lewis officiating. Rev. K. M. Kerrick, pastor of the First Baptist Church assisted. Burial was in Throckmorton Cemetery under the direction of Merriman Funeral Home.

Grable, born March 18, 1880 in Parker County, had lived here for the past 35 years. He was a member of the Methodist Church here for more than 25 years.

Survivors include his wife of Throckmorton; a son, John A. Grable of Throckmorton; two daughters, Mrs. Thomas Boyd of Throckmorton and Mrs. Joseph Jurlina of Cleveland, Ohio; two sisters, seven brothers and five grandchildren.

Hospital Notes

Visiting hours at the hospital are as follows: Mornings- 10:00 to 11:00; Afternoons- 2:00 to 4:00; and Evenings- 7:00 to 9:00.

Mrs. Henry Hext, admitted 3-27, dismissed 3-31.

Mrs. Mattie Beown, dismissed 3-31.

Mr. J. F. Grable, admitted 3-29, passed away 3-30.

THROCKMORTON TRIBUNE

OBITUARY

JOHN ROBERT GRABLE

John Robert Grable , Ed. D., son of deceased parents John A. Grable and Beaulah Low (Lee) Grable, passed away at his home in College Station, Texas on May 19, 2007. His father was a well known rancher and his mother taught in the Elementary School in Throckmorton for many years.

John R. was a graduate of Throckmorton High School, attended North Texas University, University of New Mexico, and Texas A&M University. He taught in the Abilene Schools for several years and served as President of Brazosport College in Lake Jackson, Texas. Active in civic endeavors , he was a member of the Aggieland Rotary Club and volunteered at the Bush Library. He also served in the Navy, where he reached the rank of Lieutenant.

Dr. Grable is survived by his wife, Carol Belknap Grable of College Station; a son, John Grable and wife, Pamela, of Clute, Texas; two daughters , Leslie McGinnis and husband, Kevin, of College Station, and Susan Shipley and husband, Jeff, of Woodlands, Texas; one brother, Jerry Lee and wife, Claire Grable of Dallas, Texas, an Aunt Billie Grable Jurlina and her husband Joseph, Cousins Carol Ann Krumm and Michael Jurlina of Richardson, Texas; Cousins Bobby and Tommy Boyd of Throckmorton, Texas. He is also survived by eight grandchildren, Abram and Jacye Grable, Taylor, Reagan and Payton McGinnis, and Katherine, Matthew and Caroline Shipley.

The funeral service was held on Thursday, May 24, 2007 at 10:00 a.m. at A&M United Methodist Church with Rev. Kip Gilts officiating. Burial followed at College Station Cemetery.

The family requests that memorials be made to the American Cancer Society; A&M United Methodist Church, 317 University Drive, College Station, Texas 77840; or Hospice Brazos Valley, 502 W. 26th, Bryan, Texas 77803.

Vick Cousins: Kathryn Howell, Rouye Rush, and Billie

BEULAH LOW GRABLE
DEC. 20. 1906
MAR. 17. 1994

JOHN F. GRABLE
MAR. 4, 1880
MAR. 30, 1952

WILLIE L. GRABLE
OCT. 6, 1887
OCT. 2, 1960

Parents of Billie & Kurline & Brother of Bill

JOHN A. GRABLE
DEC. 5, 1904
OCT. 29, 1952

My Uncle Virgle (Victor) Grable

0 CENTS
PAY NO MORE

VOLUME LXXXIX—NO. 34

Chicago Sunday Tribune

THE WORLD'S GREATEST NEWSPAPER

AUGUST 21, 1930.

A *

PRICE TEN CENTS

FINAL EDITION

150,000 HEAR FEAST OF SONG

THE CHICAGOLAND MUSIC FESTIVAL.

Victor Grabel has been the General musical Director of this greatest of national musical events since its inception. In addition to directing his band which is the only professional and official band of the festival; he has selected the programs, alloted the time given contestants and events, made arrangements of special numbers, assisted in the judging of contests, and planned all of the outside attractions introduced each year.

Many people do not realize the magnitude of this great Music Festival. Three times it has broken the world's record of 100,000 attendance established by the meeting of the International Choral Union at Vienna in 1929. The grand average for the period of its existence totals in excess of 120,000. The greatest throng ever to attend the Festival or any other such an event greatly exceeded the capacity of Soldiers Field when 150,000 people filled every seat, and every inch of standing room; while 30,000 people could not gain admittance and were turned away.

Much of the success of these Festivals is credited to the musical ability

Musician of High Merit.

In welcoming brilliant guest conductors, however, it must not be forgotten that the Chicagoland Music Festival has in its town conductor a musician of high merit. He is Victor Grabel, band leader and general musical director of the Chicagoland Music Festivals since the series started.

A former associate of Mr. Sousa at Great Lakes Naval Training station during the war, Mr. Grabel was one of the first bandmasters to cross the ocean with the American forces. He is secretary of the American Band-masters' association. In itself a mark of his ability, since no one is permitted to join the association without a complete equipment as musician and leader. A wise and far seeing organizer and director, he has put all his efforts into the Chicagoland Music Festival programs and has been greatly responsible for their success and influence.

On Saturday night he will present for the first time on these programs a brilliant cornet soloist, Ernest F. Pechin.

6. A dramatic performance of Tschaikowsky's famous "1812", overture by the festival band of 100 under the direction of Victor Grabel, the music augmented by cannon, spectacular fireworks, and the great carillon of bells of the Century of Progress exposition.

7. Massed bands 2,000 strong, playing Sousa marches under Mr. Grabel's direction.

There will also be the three prize winning choruses, men's, women's, and mixed, likewise the two prize winning bands, adult and juvenile, and the prize winning soloist. Further, more, Mr. Grabel and the festival band will present a new composition for the first time on any stage.

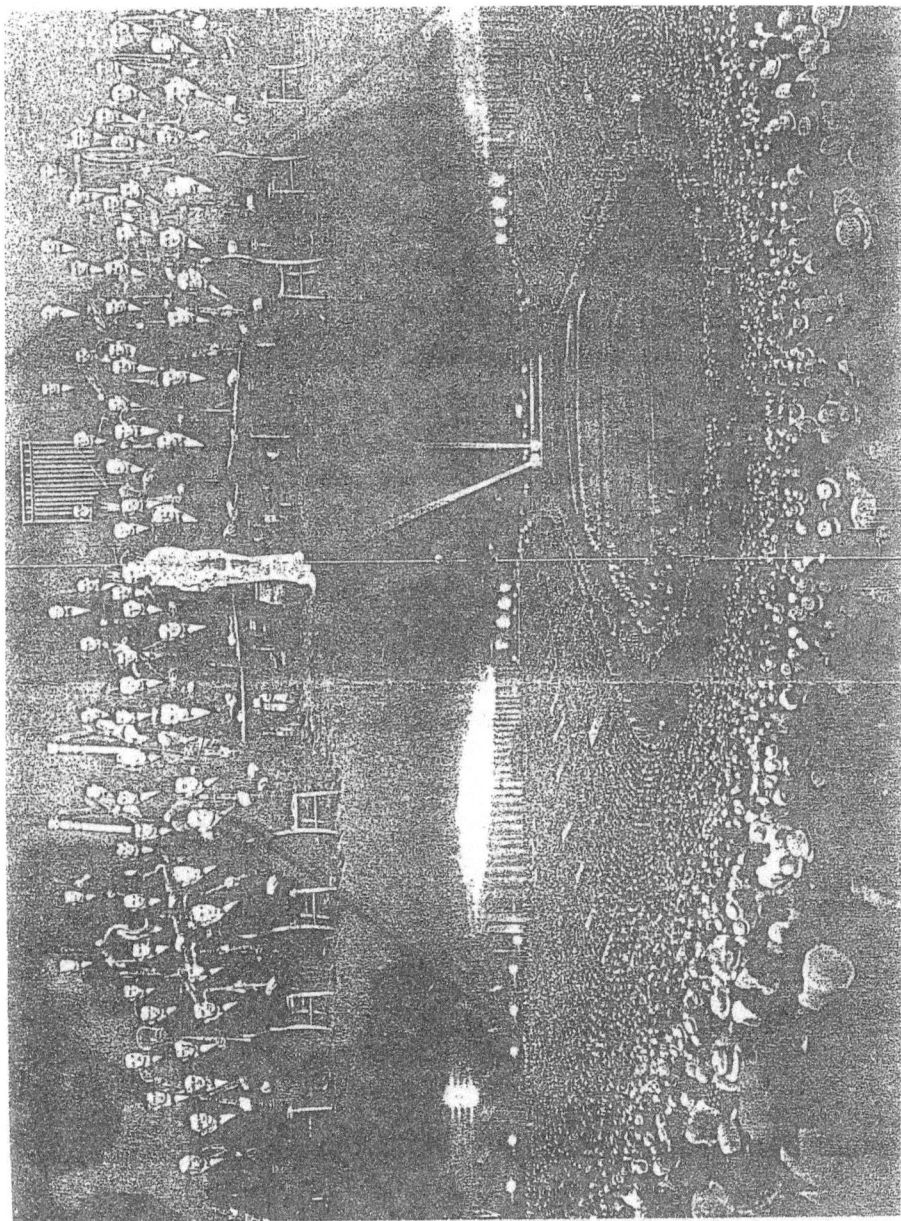

BAND TONE UP GRANT PARK

BY HERMA?

Nothing daunted by post-prandial showers and the threat of storm, the Chicago Concert Band Association opened a series of concerts in Grant Park last night to the applause of an audience seemingly aware of the quality of the music as well as of the generous intention of its sponsors.

BAND'S TONE UNIMPAIRED.

Last night's opening program was happily chosen and received with every mark of favor. In spite of the open spaces, the tone of the band, under the expert leadership of Victor Grabel, as well as the voice of the assisting solo soprano, Miss Rosalinda Morini, was unimpaired, and I am safe in the hope that the series of 1931 will be a successful augury for the future of the organization.

We were prepared for the excellence of the band's accomplishments, for we had heard the men rehearse at the Auditorium during their period of preparation and even then their performance was a joy. The pleasure was augmented last night by the surety and finish of their execution, the resonance and richness of the instrumental blend, and the verve and resiliency of their response to Mr. Grabel's musical will.

I particularly enjoyed their playing of the Massenet "Cid" ballet. Here was genuine band rhythm, stimulating and zestful. A tour de force must also be praised. The Siegfried "Death March," which I heard from a considerable distance; purposely to gauge the carrying possibilities of the open-air band, was remarkably fine.

Other things on the program were a' Saint-Saens' military march, excerpts from the Strauss "Choco-

Opera Features Band Concert by Victor Grabel

By Glenn Dillard Gunn.

AN OPERATIC OBSESSION has descended upon the military bands of America. Victor Grabel's Chicago Concert Band, playing last night in Grant Park, represented this form of the musical uplift with the prelude to "Die Meistersinger" and the funeral march from "Die Goetterdaemmerung" of Wagner, with the ballet music from Massenet's "Le Cid" to console the musically light-minded.

The soloist, the efficient Rosalinda Morini, charming coloratura, was scheduled to sing excerpts from "Mignon" and "Il Re Pastore" of Mozart. Lighter numbers listed included Grabel's own march, "Fair Chicago." A word of praise is due Mr. Grabel, not only for the inclusion of the finale from Tschaikowsky's fourth symphony, but for the footnote in the program which admonished the listener who may have been pleased with this number to hear it in its entirety when next played by the Chicago Symphony.

* * *

CONDUCTOR GRABEL, who was discovered by the late John Philip Sousa and energetically promoted by him, has been a leader in the development of high school bands throughout the country through the medium of contests. He organized the first of such nationwide contests nine years ago. Now, it is estimated by the Bureau for the Advancement of Music, that there are 20,000 school bands in America with a membership of 1,500,000.

GRabie

Victor Grabel greeting John Philip Sousa and Mrs. Sousa upon Mr. Sousa's arrival to be guest conductor of the Chicago Concert Band at the Chicagoland Music Festival of 1931.

Uncle Virgle/changed his name To Victor /Virgel/

VICTOR JEAN GRABEL.

Victor Grabel was born near Prairieville, Texas.

When fifteen he started the study of music, cornet being his chosen instrument.

He was studying at Texas Christian University when Sousa's Band came to town. This event altered the course of his life. It so fired him with the determination to become a band conductor that he gave up the study of Law and immediately enrolled at Dana's Musical Institute in Warren, Ohio.

When Professor H. Clark Thayer, Director of the Band Department left to become President of Susquehanna College of Music at Clearfield, Pa., young Grabel went with him. To pay expenses he assisted in teaching, and played local professional engagements.

Four years of uninterrupted study caused his health to fail, so he enlisted in the 7th Infantry Band at Detroit in order to secure more of an outdoor life. During this period he travelled over a large part of this country, and to many places in the Orient.

Later he directed the 3rd Regiment Band at Hillsboro, Texas, and the State Vocational Band at Lansing, Michigan.

In 1914 Mr. Grabel organized his famous Chicago Band which occupied his time until war was declared in 1917.

When the war broke out, Grabel immediately enrolled in the Navy, where he soon began to attract national attention. At his own expense he recruited a fine concert band that was soon the pride of the Great Lakes Station. This band played in many of the leading cities of the country. When the Navy Department wanted to send a crack band aboard the U.S.S. Pennsylvania, the flagship of the Atlantic Fleet, Sousa wired them to "get Grabel", and they got Grabel. The concerts of that band both afloat and ashore led critics to acclaim it as the finest service band in the United States. One of the recordings of that band became one of the Columbia Graphophone Company's "best sellers". This band was also the only service band mentioned by the late John Philip Sousa in his book of Memoirs "Keeping Time".

Immediately after being mustered out of the service Mr. Grabel accepted the directorship of the Municipal Band at Danville, Illinois.

He next accepted the position as head of the Music Department of the Western Electric Company of Chicago, one of the largest industrial institutions in the world. For five years he remained with this company playing noon concerts with his sixty piece band and giving concerts at Orchestra Hall which drew capacity houses.

Mr. Grabel then formed the Chicago Concert Band made up of the finest musicians obtainable. It is this band that the critics have acclaimed as one of the finest ever assembled anywhere at anytime. This band has achieved a definite place in the musical life of Chicago and the Midwest; and Mr. Grabel proudly offers it to the public as his greatest achievement.

In addition to his band activities Mr. Grabel contributes to eleven periodicals. Some of his articles have attracted favorable comment from leading executives of the Nation. For the past eleven years he has edited the Band and Orchestra Department of The Etude, the world's predominant music magazine.

Mr. Grabel is one of the founders of the American Bandmasters Association and has continually held office in that organization.

Mr. Grabel organized the first National High School Band Contest in 1925, and has judged regularly at District, State and National Contests. Every year he fills a number of engagements as Guest Conductor at Band Clinics in various parts of the country.

Mr. Grabel is also widely known as a composer and arranger. His compositions have been played by many famous organizations, and have received much favorable comment from the critics. As an arranger, and especially for large concert bands, he has few equals.

He was a warm personal friend of the late John Philip Sousa to whom he stands indebted for much help and kindly advice. Through Mr. Grabel's efforts a Sousa Memorial Association has recently been formed to honor the memory of Mr. Sousa.

Mr. Grabel owns, in addition to his fine large library, the original library of the Sousa Band, which was presented to him in 1931 by Mr. Sousa

Drum Throbs Open Festival Tonight

James O'Donnell Bennett

This is about uncle Virgle Grable — (handwritten)

Builds Up Adroit Finale.

The finale that now is enveloping us is that opulent blending of prayer and of battle, Tschaikowsky's overture, "1812.".

Grabel is holding his men well together. The big spectacular passages are going over with enormous effect. Now the brazen clamor of the church bells tolling the doom of Moscow. Now the bombardment from the battery of artillery far away on the lake front.

It is far away but it is so heavy that the tiers of cement seats tremble under it. You can actually feel the concussion.

Thrilled Audience Cheers.

Excitement mounts. The audience is cheering in the midst of the music.

Grabel gives the electric signal for the release of bombs and rockets. To the east the dark, cloudless sky blazes with them.

The cannonade continues amid the booming of the bronze bells, the roll of drums, and the wild screaming of the trumpets.

Bravo, Grabel! You are getting out of the piece every thrill there is in it and you are carrying your auditors along with you. They are praying with the Russians; they are exulting with Napoleon.

Mighty Setting Is Factor.

The secret of the prodigious effect lies not altogether in the proficiency and certainty of the musicians. Again —as all through this illustrious evening—the mighty setting is a factor.

For when you can release the "1812" at the end of a cañon of concrete and fling it for an eighth of a mile through that cañon and when you have a Greek temple for your sounding board—and the sky for your canopy——then you have an auditorium that is worthy of the music of battle and of triumph.

Grabel was very adroit in building up an unexpected featural finale. "1812" having ended, he, with hardly a breath of intermission, carried the 150,000 into "My Country, 'Tis of Thee"—the remote cannon—ah, that remoteness was subtly grand!—still booming, the sky still flaming with fire, the drums still beating, and the bells still tolling.

The exultant multitude — excited, thrilled, inspired, rose to the bandsmen and their leader.

Bands from as far east as the Wabash and from across the Mississippi, swung into time with the official festival band. Eleven hundred men were playing.

The thousands on the Dot sang of their land, its rocks and rills, this land where their fathers died, this land of the Pilgrims' austere pride.

An Abiding Inspiration.

On this note of consecration the night ended.

The circling garlands of lights sank to a red glow, then into darkness. The search lamps withdrew their white shafts from the canopy of sky. The glittering bands—still playing, but playing now those fleeting tunes of the day that make the people smile while humming the easy refrains—marched blithely off the field.

The standards of the states and the flags of the republic sank from their masts.

The festival was over. It leaves memory and an inspiration that will abide.

"Music" said the genial Berthold Auerbach, "washes away from the soul the dust of everyday life."

That is what has happened last night. That is why the people wended their homeward way refreshed and joyful.

Chicago Tribune.

"Victor Grabel gave the most dramatic and musicianly interpretation of the Il Guarany overture I have ever heard."

—*Herman Devries,*
Chicago Evening American.

"He is a genial host whose promise of a palatable musical feast is most bountifully fulfilled."

—*Evening Telegram, New York.*

"The work of Mr. Grabel's band in the principal program numbers was truly artistic—often approximating the coloring and *finesse* of a symphony orchestra. When it swings into the measures of a military march, it is stirring, brilliant."

—*Chicago Evening Post.*

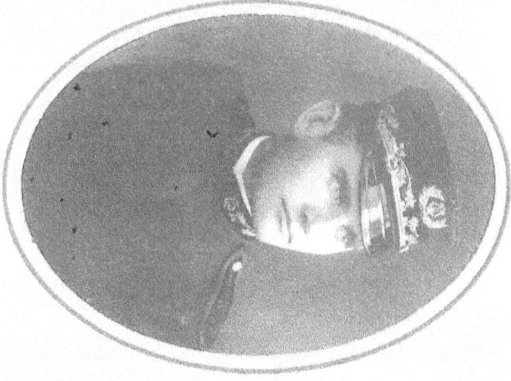

VIRGIL JEAN GRABLE
B. 1 FEB 1886
D. 13 JUNE 1965

MEMBER OF JOHN PHILIP SOUSA
BAND

Also formed his own
marching band in
Chicago

Perrin Woman Celebrates 81st Birthday in Throckmorton.

Mrs. J. F. Grable and Mrs. J. L. Brown of Throckmorton were co-hostesses at a dinner given in the home of Mrs. Grable for her mother, Mrs. N. M. Vick of Perrin, who was celebrating her 81st birthday. Billie John Grable and Kathryne Brown were also honorees as their birthdays also come in September. The table was beautifully decorated with cut flowers and ferns, and centered with a large three-tier birthday cake with 81 lighted tapers. Mrs. Vick was greeted in the dining room by the singing of "Happy Birthday," and when seated at the table the honoree's children, grand-children and great-grand-children presented her with many beautiful and useful gifts.

Approximately thirty guests enjoyed this happy occasion—coming from all directions in many parts of Texas and some from Arkansas.

Jurlina's celebrate 60 years of marriage

Joseph and Billie Jurlina

Joseph and Billie Grable Jurlina celebrated with family and friends at a reception held in their honor at St. Luke's Episcopal Church on May 29, 2005. While serving with the U.S. Army in Denton, Joe, originally from Cleveland, Ohio, met Billie from Throckmorton who was attending North Texas State Teacher's College. They were married May 12, 1945 at the First Methodist Church in Wichita Falls.

After graduating in 1950 from the University of Texas at Austin in Electrical Engineering, Joe returned to Cleveland to design machinery for Process Machine and Tool Co., for manufacture of the Walker Bulldog T-41-E1 Tank used in the Korean War. In 1952 the family returned to Dallas where Joe began a 35 year career with Texas Power & Light Company including positions as Sherman District Manager and Manager of Systems Engineering before his retirement in 1987. He was a member of the Texas Society of Professional Engineers and IEEE. Billie taught Home Economics for 22 years in the Richardson Independent School District, and in 1984 was selected as "Texas Home Economics Teacher of the Year."

Their children and spouses are Carol Ann and William E. Krumm of Richardson and Michael K. and Pamela Jurlina of Dallas. They have four grandchildren and three great grandchildren.

Appendix C:
Diary of 1st Trip to England- Summer of 1982

While we were still working, we made two trips to England. We went with JoAnn Bell who was Richardson schools library consultant and an anglophile. She planned and executed the trips. The first trip was with Jim and Glenie Byron, John and Marge Kloeppel, Will and JoAnn Bell and Joe and me. On June 4, 1982, Mike took us to DFW Airport where we flew to England on a D-C 10 British Caldonian airliner. We had made reservations three months prior to the flight requesting NO-SMOKING seats, but it did no good. I was in the middle of the smoking section. (Joe said I was seeing the British caste system at work.) After landing at Gatwick, we picked up the two white Ford station wagons we had reserved to travel in. The first place we visited was Winston Churchill's home, Chartwell. The grounds were beautiful. We left Chartwell about 12:30 p.m. going to Six Mile Bottom. We stopped at Black Horse Pub in Farningham for lunch. We progressed along through Dartmoor Tunnel (goes under the Thames River).

Our reservations at Swynford Paddocks were wonderful. This was the former home of Lord Byron's half sister, Augusta Leigh, having been given to her husband in 1809 by the Prince of Wales whose race horses were managed by her husband, Colonel Leigh. Dinner was served in the dining room at 8:15. The setting was both romantic and beautiful. Candles and flower bouquets graced the tables. The food was delicious and the service was formal and immaculate. They had a trolley of tempting desserts. Following dinner, coffee was served in the lounge. Joe and I walked around the grounds under a full moon.

Sunday, June 6, we drove to Cambridge. Mr. James Melanby was our guide on a walking tour for 2 1/2 hours. He was a retired 82 year old engineer of Scottish descent—a very interesting fellow. We had a bite of lunch at the Copper Kettle across the street from King's College. We walked across a bridge and watched the college kids rowing boats on the Cam River. We attended Evensong at Kings Chapel on the Kings College campus. The boy's choir was magnificent. After evensong, the boys left the building in top hats and formal wear. It was still daylight so we went to Ely and saw Ely Cathedral. It is huge and very beautiful.

Monday, June 7th, we had breakfast, checked out of the hotel and drove to Thetford. We saw a statue of Thomas Paine in front of the Council House (City Hall) that the people of New York had donated. We went on to Norwich, visited the castle keep, and museum. We had tea in the Buttery. We walked over to Norich Cathedral and saw a slide commentary and learned about the misericords (a small seat people could stand but recline against) to be used when the church service was l-o-n-g. We departed Norich about 3:30 p.m. driving along the North Sea. We saw lots of poppies, and lavender fields. We arrived at Duke Head's Hotel in King's Lynn about 5:30 p.m. This hotel faced on a town square where people brought their wares to sell from individual stalls. We were not into Genealogy when we made this trip. Years later when we started doing family research, we discovered that our 5th great grandfather probably came from Kings Lynn. Too bad we didn't know it when we were there. After checking out of the hotel, we drove to Walpole. St. Andrews and St. Peters churches were having their annual flower festival. The floral arrangements were exquisite.

Some of the English terms we learned include: Layby--place to pull off the highway; Car Park--parking area; Roundabout--traffic Circle; Give Way--yield; Dual Carriageway--divided freeway.

Tuesday June 8, we arrived at Burghley House at 12:20 p.m. We toured the house, ate lunch in the orangery and were on our way by 2:30. You cannot imagine the size of these houses we visited. They are called Trust Houses as they have been placed in trust to the English government. The houses and grounds are kept up by the government through what they charge for people to visit them. We stopped in Newstead Abbey to visit the home of Lord Byron. We went on to Epworth, the home of Methodism and John Wesley. We saw the Wesley memorial church and the original church of Wesley which is no longer in use. We arrived in York about 8:15 p.m. We stayed at a Trust House Hotel. The next morning (Wednesday) we took a walking tour of York. We walked along the old Roman wall which looks down on York Minster grounds. We saw The Shambles (shops), the Treasurer's House, and toured York Minster. The stained glass over the altar is as big as 4 tennis courts. It is just beautiful. We drove out to Castle Howard and toured it.

Thursday June 10, we headed for Wales via M-62. On the way, we toured Chester Cathedral which is built of red sandstone. I did some shopping at Brown's Department store in THE ROWS. I bought Mike, Carol Ann, Mary Jane and Katherine each a Royal Doulton figurine. We had lunch at a small café named "60's American Burger Bar". We traveled on to Abersock Wales. A bookstore proved to have some books JoAnn wanted. Joe feels a cold coming on. We arrived at our hotel The Porth Tocyn, about 6 p.m.

Friday June 11, we visited the castle in Carnafon, Wales. It was raining, cold and Joe was sick with a cold and raw throat. We then progressed on to Plas Newydd a Trust Fort House on Menai Strait. We saw a lot of lovely flowers. We drove back to our hotel for dinner, played bridge and to bed early. Saturday June 12, we traveled to Llyswen and checked into the Griffin Inn. We drove over to Hay-On-Wye to a book store (old issues) and an antique shop but found nothing we needed.

Sunday June 13, we headed toward Mullion Cove. On the way we stopped at Tintern Abbey, crossed the Severn River and stopped at THF service center for breakfast. We stopped in Plymouth for refreshments. We saw the Wm. Drake Monument. We arrived in Mullion Cove about 4 p.m. The name of the cottage was Traveen and it took us three or four runs to find it because someone had taken the sign down. The Cove where the cottage was situated was beautiful. Monday, June 14, we prepared breakfast, and then drove to Trerice Manor House. It was lovely. They had a tea room in an old barn where we had refreshments before driving on to the town of Tintagel. It was quaint. We got back to Mullion Cove about 6:30. Marge and JoAnn had prepared a formal English dinner for the six of us.

Tuesday, June 15, the men prepared breakfast and cleaned up the kitchen. We then drove to Penzance. We went to Land's End and saw a sign pointing to the U.S.A. with the mileage which I can't remember. We drove to St. Ives, a lovely coastal town. We shopped at The New Craftsman Shop. I bought a small wooden shoe box with a slide out brass top. It was made by Alexander Woodcock out of 80 year old mahogany. It could also be used to hold a secret note or snuff. I brought this back to Mike because when he was in the military service overseas, he collected several beautiful small boxes. We ate lunch at The Beach Restaurant upstairs overlooking St. Ives Bay. On our way back to the cottage, we stopped in Mullion to buy groceries. We had to go to a bakery for bread; meat market for meat; dairy market for milk, clotted cream, etc.; and two different grocery stores for fresh vegetables and fruit. People had to take their own sacks or boxes to carry their food home. Glenie and I prepared dinner. After dinner, I sat in the living room listening to the rain while reading. The book, My Cousin Rachael, by Daphne DuMaurier was very interesting as the setting is in Cornwall England. Many of the towns and places we have visited are mentioned in the book. Everyone went to bed except me. I saw something move out of the corner of my eye which proved to be a small mouse. This was a perfect English setting for reading this book.

Wednesday, June 16, we drove to Lizard Point after breakfast. This is the most southerly point in England. We arrived in Marazion about 10:00 a.m. We rode a small ferry (12 people max.) out to St. Michael's Mount. We saw a fifteen minute film and then walked up the mount to the top of the Castle and toured the castle. I can't imagine living on top of a small mountain back in that time. When we returned to Marazion, we had lunch at a darling little restaurant overlooking Mount's Bay. After lunch, we drove to Porthcurno to see the dress rehearsal of <u>King Arthur</u> at the Minick (open air) Theatre. It is situated so that the audience is facing the beautiful Atlantic Ocean. On the way back to the cottage, we stopped at The Potters Wheel gift shop and bought a few things. I still use two of the coasters purchased there.

Thursday, June 17, we left the cottage hoping to see the gardens at Glendurgan, but they were not open that particular day. We went on to Trelissick Gardens and had coffee and scones. We took a ferry across to St. Mawes and lunch at the Rising Sun Inn before going up to St. Mawes Castle. We progressed to Truro and visited the Truro Cathedral. We returned to the cottage for dinner. We packed to leave the cottage the next morning. Staying in this cottage was interesting. It had three bedrooms, two baths, a kitchen and eating area and a living room. We had to put quarters in a meter to get electricity and in another meter to get water in addition to the rent for a week. It was a lovely experience.

Friday, June 18, we left Trevean headed for Blockley. The sun was shining after a night of heavy rain. It was cool. We had to get petrol which cost 12.75 pounds for 34.27 liters. We took route A30 to Indian Queens. We saw slides and photographs of clay tips. This is the area where they obtain clay for making fine china. (It is disintegrated granite they say) We stopped at the Jamacia Inn and had coffee and a cookie at the Smuggler's bar. This Inn is the setting for Daphne DuMaurier's book titled Jamacia Inn. We stopped in Chagfort for lunch at Three Crowns Bar. The food served in Bars was very good. We arrived in Blockley at 5p.m. and checked into Lower Brook House. Our rooms were upstairs and very nice. We walked around the gardens and grounds before dinner. We called granddaughter, Katherine, for her birthday.

Saturday, June 19, we drove over to Chipping Campden. Most all of the buildings are constructed of honey colored stone which is indigenous to the Cotswold area. We visited St. James Parish Church and the surrounding burial grounds. We drove out to Hidcote gardens which were lovely. We progressed on to Broughton to visit the home of Lady Sele and Lord Saye. The Lord is the brother of the Dean of Lincoln Cathedral whom the Byrons had met at Church of the Transfiguration in Dallas. The home was very large and also very beautiful. It was in the open country so the lovely grounds were quite effective.

Returning to our hotel, we changed clothes and went into Stratford. We went to the Shakespeare Theatre and saw "MUCH ADO ABOUT NOTHING". We had to walk across a bridge over the Avon River to get to and from the theatre. We watched a houseboat go through the locks. We enjoyed seeing that as it was quite interesting. The stage in the theatre slanted toward the audience which was great as you had no trouble seeing the rear of the stage. The tables and chairs had shorter back legs to accommodate the slanting stage. Plastic rectangles with trees painted on them were used as curtain drops. They were very effective. We returned to our rooms at Lower Brook House and had a midnight dinner. The LBH was a lovely place to stay. Our rooms were upstairs overlooking a lovely garden. Roses were climbing up the walls and were in full bloom.

Sunday, June 20, Joe got a long distance call from our children back in the USA wishing him a Happy Father's Day. That really surprised him. We checked out of Lower Brook House and arrived in Uffington to see the White Horse on the Hill. This mysterious horse was cut into the chalk hillside. The origin of this white horse remains a mystery, but some think it is of the Iron Age while others believe it is Saxon. During World War II, the horse was covered with mud and straw to prevent it from being bombed by the Germans. The location was also denied to the enemy. We went on to Stonehenge where a Druid

Festival was in progress. I suppose the festival could be described as the HIPPY FESTIVAL of Los Angeles back in the sixties—drugs and strange dress were prevalent. Stonehenge is a circle of huge stones and was used as an outdoor temple, ceremonial meeting place and burial ground. The stones are about 14 feet high, and have a tongue & groove method holding a lintel stone across the top of every two stones. It was quite interesting to see. We drove into Salisbury and attended 3 p.m. matins at the cathedral. We left Salisbury about 4 p.m. for Winchester. We toured Winchester Cathedral. It is huge and beautiful. We pressed on to Rushlake Green arriving at Priory House about 8:15 where we had reservations. We got to our rooms, freshened up a bit and went back to the lounge to order dinner. We had coffee and dessert in the lounge after dinner and then to bed.

Monday, June 21, after a luscious breakfast, we went to Rye. We parked in Cattle Car Park and walked up Rope Walk to "Lamb House" for a tour of the house and garden. Both were interesting and lovely. We drove on to Sam and Jessica Youd's home. Sam is an author whom Jo Anne had met here in Richardson. Jessica had prepared a lovely lunch for us. Their home was unusual in that it was long, narrow and four stories high. We enjoyed our time with these unusual and interesting people. Jessica died about two years after our visit. We saw St. Mary's church, visited the famous MERMAID Inn which was rebuilt in 1635 (or close to it). The doorway was about five feet tall, the floors were so uneven you could hardly stand upright, but it certainly was a historic site. We saw the town model of Rye which was very interesting. We paid a visit to an antique shop and a pottery shop. We then returned to Rushlake Green and our rooms at the Priory House to freshen up for dinner. We had a lovely dinner at the War-Bill-In-Tun Pub. It was large and rather fancy. The chairs were upholstered in maroon velvet. The dessert was served in tall sundae glasses. It was vanilla ice cream with strawberries, nuts and whipped cream mixed in. They put a huge "top hat" of meringue on top. After coffee, we returned to Priory House and watched a movie on the "telle". Lady Dianna had given birth to Prince William at 9:03 that evening so the news was all over television. All the Brits were very excited about the birth as were we.

Tuesday, June 22, we rose early to what we thought would be a sunny day, but a couple of hours later it started to rain. We arrived for a 10 a.m. tour of Bateman House. It was lovely. On we went to Brighton. We toured the Royal Pavilion and museum. It was very exotic. Brighton is an interesting town of spectacular contrasts. Graceful Georgian and late-Victorian houses co-exist with the extravaganza of the Royal Pavilion. The blend of culture and candy floss is Brighton's fascination. The village by the sea became famous when in the mid 18th century Dr. Richard Russell proclaimed the health values of sea bathing and breathing sea air. The Prince of Wales, son of George III, visited Brighton in 1783 and commissioned Henry Holland to build him a ROYAL PAVILLION there in classical style with a "Chinese" interior. When the Prince became Regent in 1812 he engaged John Nash, the architect who laid our Regent's Park in London and the terraces round it, to enlarge the Pavilion into the present riotously extravagant building. It has an onion shaped dome and minarets in the style of an Indian Prince's palace. It faces the Black Sea and a long boardwalk is at the seafront. Brighton soon became the leading resort in England. Today, modern Brighton is still one of Britain's leading seaside resorts. It has one of the largest yacht marinas in Europe. All year round 5,000 business men and women travel by train into London and back. The University of Suxxex, on the outskirts of Brighton, has added a new dimension to the town's life, including a modern theatre, the Gardner Centre. The students' lodging places, east of the town centre double as seaside holiday flats during the summer vacation. Brighton has a flourishing cultural life, centered on the Theatre Royal, whose productions are up to London standards. There is an arts festival in May and a permanent concert hall, the Dome. The art gallery and museum is one of England's finest.

We had lunch at "For Fars" located in The Lanes. We returned to The Priory and received a call from Mike which was nice. We had dinner at the War Bill In-Tun pub.

Wednesday, June 23, 1982, we left The Priory at Rushing Green and headed for London. We had driven a total of 2,619 miles. In London, we turned in the rental car, and checked into our rooms at Searcy's Roof Garden Hotel. It is a small hotel above a catering/party place. It is very close to Harrods. At 5p.m. we went to the Grenadier Pub for dinner. We then walked about two miles to the Haymarket Theatre to see a live production of Amadeus (the story of Mozart's life).

Thursday, June 24, we walked over to see the Changing of the Guard at the Palace. We met Patsy German (a fellow teacher from Northwood Jr. High) who was living in London because her husband had been transferred there. We met Gene German at Ye Old Cheshire Cheese Pub for lunch. The Pub is on the third floor and looks to be 150 years old. After lunch, Patsy and Gene went their way and we went to tour St. Paul's Cathedral. After the tour, we took a cab to Westminster Abbey; saw the Parliament buildings and St. Margaret's Chapel where parliament members worship. We ate dinner across the street from Harrods at the French Brasserie. Back to Searcy's and to bed.

Friday, June 25, we had breakfast delivered to our room. Then we walked over to Parliament as we had tickets to attend a session of the House of Commons. The arguing between the parties is just as we see it on TV sometimes. We then walked down Victoria Street to the Army Navy store to purchase souvenirs. After taking our packages back to our hotel, we took a cab to the Tower of London to see the Crown Jewels. We had dinner at a downtown Holiday Inn and then we walked over to Hyde Park. We passed the building which had a plaque on the front saying U.S. President Kennedy lived there from 1961-1963. We turned down Exposition St., passed through a college campus and saw the outside of The Albert and Victoria Museum. Maybe we can see the inside next trip. The four night stay including breakfast each day was l00.28 pounds. That is equal to about $60.00 US money.

Saturday, June 26, we were up at 4:30 to dress and get our taxis out to Gatwick Airport by 6:30a.m. BRITISH CALDONIAN AIRLINES had canceled our flight (thank goodness) so we were put on AMERICAN AIRLINES. What a difference in our flight back to the states. The movie, Chariots of Fire, was shown during the flight. We landed at DFW at 4p.m. As we walked into the terminal, we saw Bill & Carol Ann and Jason and Katherine. When we reached customs, there stood Mike to greet us. We got home about 5:15 and the grandchildren had put up crepe paper and a "WELCOME HOME" sign. All the lights were on and they had brought sandwich makings and cold drinks so we had a good visit and distributed their souvenirs. How wonderful to be welcomed by our children. We were in bed by 10 p.m. trying to catch up with the jet lag....

Appendix D:
Diary of 2nd Trip to England- Summer of 1985

Jo Anne Bell planned this trip too. She and five teachers, Glenie and Jim Byron, and Joe and I went on this trip. We rented three Ford Wagons, one was red, one was blue and one was white. The Byrons' and Jurlinas' did not always travel with the girls during the day, but met up at night at our hotels.

July 2, 1985 Carol Ann, Jason and Katherine drove us to the DFW airport to get our plane to London. Our American Pilot Son got us bumped up to first class so our trip was wonderful. We were served a seven course meal with appropriate wines. I had Lobster Thermador. To top off the delicious meal, they served Hagan Daz hot fudge sundaes. We were able to sleep some and were up at 5 a.m. for a lovely breakfast on July 3rd. We landed at Gatwick at 7 a.m. After going through customs, we rode the express train into London. We got a taxi to Searcy's rooms. We unpacked, took a nap and went over to Harrod's. Joe bought a "Book of the Road" to use in our travels. This trip was to see Castles and Gardens. After Glenie and Jim Byron arrived, we went to The Albert and Victoria Museum. It is so wonderful that words are difficult to find to describe it. We went back to Searcys to take a nap before dinner at Wolfe's.

Thursday, July 4, we had a lovely breakfast before walking to the Embankment to ride the Zodiac up the Thames River to Greenwich and the barrier reefs. This was quite educational and we did a lot of photographing. We had lunch at The Clarence Pub. We went to the Royal Courts of Justice. It was neat to see the lawyers in their robes and white wigs. We rode the "tube" back to Searcy's. About 5:30 we dressed to go to New London Theatre where we saw "CATS". I loved it, but Joe didn't care for any of it except the song Memories. It was interesting when at intermission, I got up to go to the restroom and met a teacher (Susie Snodgrass) from Richardson High School where we both taught. Small World! There were a few American Flags flying around London which we found neighborly.

Friday, July 5, we walked to Victoria Station and caught a train to Rochester. Glenie and JoAnn had met Mr. Reives of Reives China in the U.S. His shop is on Hight Street. Of course, we had to order a few pieces of china. Then we walked over to Rochester Cathedral where I did two brass rubbings (for Carol Ann and Mike) which I had framed and gave to them for Christmas. We had lunch about 2:30 at Peggity's Tea Room. It was located on the second floor of a building overlooking the Cathedral Grounds. We left for London by train about 4:30 P.M. We had dinner at Wolfe's, came back to our rooms and played Shanghai Rummy with the Byrons until bedtime.

Saturday, July 6, it is cool and sunny. The rain in London yesterday really cooled things off. Today, we caught the train out to Hatfield House. Queen Elizabeth lst grew up in the original Palace here. Part of it has been torn away and is now a Carriage Museum. Our friend, Ed Veigel spent some time in Hatfield House (turned into a hospital during WWII) recuperating from his shrapnel wounds received in his legs, hands (and blinded him in one eye eventually). Ed was the navigator on a B-17 (Flying Fortress) and they flew several missions over Germany. We rode the train back to London, had dinner at Wolfe's and then took a taxi to the Apollo Victoria theatre to see "Starlight Express". We left at intermission because we didn't care for it though the engineering, logistics and skating were phenomenal.

Sunday, July 7, we went to Holy Trinity Church on Sloane Street near the square. Not many people were in attendance. The building and the stained glass windows were beautiful. We went to the train station and rode out to Kew Gardens. KEW contains the world-famous botanical gardens, 286 acres in extent, partly landscaped by Capability Brown for King George III and opened to the public in 1841. The Palm House, forerunner of the Crystal Palace, was erected in 1844. It is created of iron framework and 45,000 square feet of glass. It contained many different types of blooming plants. We took so many photographs we can't count them. We had lunch in a small cafeteria near The Pagoda. After an evening snack, Joe and I walked through part of Hyde Park where a band concert was in progress.

Monday, July 8, it was partly cloudy. We were leaving London and heading for Isle of Wight by way of Portsmouth. We saw the ship HMS Victory. We went to Southampton to Dock 7 and boarded the ferry and arrived at The Isle of Wight about 4:30 p.m. Our rooms at Peacock Vane in Bonnchurch, Isle of Wight were ready for us and were beautiful. Dinner was served at 8 p.m. Joe and I went for a walk after dinner. Made it to bed about 10:30 p.m.

Tuesday, July 9, Joe and I walked down the hill to the English Channel before breakfast. After breakfast we went to Osborne House. This was Queen Victoria's home at the time of her death in 1901. Prince Albert and Thomas Cubitt designed it as an Italian villa. The house was used as a place where injured veterans could recover during WWII. About ¾ of a mile from Osborne House, a Swiss Cottage was built for the King and Queen's two children. Everything was built in miniature including wagons and gardening tools. The gardens and flowers around the estate were gorgeous. We drove into Yarmouth for snacks and tea. Dinner was served at eight. After dinner we walked down the hill and across the street to Joan Wolfenden's book store. (Joan owns Peacock Vane also) I purchased a book, entitled TheGlory of the Garden. She wrote it by hand and also did the illustrations.

Wednesday, July 10, we checked out after breakfast and rode the ferry back to Southampton. From there we drove to Oxford. It was hot there and we were tired so we didn't get to really see and enjoy the place. We did walk onto the University Campus. I walked into the Radcliffe Camera library (although no one but students were allowed inside) It really is beautiful and was built in 1737-48. We left Oxford for Waddeston Manor in Alesbury. It is a country mansion of French Renaissance style set in 160 acres of parkland, built for Baron Ferdinand de Rothschild in 1877-89. The contents include 18th century French furniture, carpets, Sevres porcelain, and paintings by Gainesborough, Reynolds, Rubens, and Dutch and Italian Schools. There is an aviary of rococo design with a variety of exotic birds. The huge gardens around the house were lovely. At the beginning of the drive into the property was a large manmade pond with several fountains flowing over pieces of statuary. It was perfectly beautiful. We had tea and scones in the tearoom. We left there at 5:40 for Moreton-in-Marsh in Glostershire. We had a room at the manor house on the third floor. It overlooked the patio and gardens below. Joyce Tomlinson and Dorislee Hoffpauer surprised us by coming over to see us and we had coffee in the lounge after dinner by the huge fireplace. They were traveling around England and had our itinerary so they decided to surprise us and pay us a visit. It was great to see them. I taught with them at Northwood Jr. High.

Thursday, July 11, after having a lovely breakfast at our inn, we drove on to Stoke-on-Trent. We had lunch at The Swan Pub. We went on to

The Royal Doulton factory for a two hour tour. The artists that paint the figurines sit at a small desk and work for 8 hours. They have a short lunch and a break in the morning and afternoon. I can't imagine doing that beautiful art work under those conditions. We then visited Johnson Brothers and Coalport. We had the opportunity to purchase seconds at Johnson Brothers but we declined. We drove on to Moreton Hall which is a half-timbered trust house. It was being revamped to prevent further deterioration. It was drizzling rain and cold so we visited their tearoom and had hot tea and scones. We drove to Congleton and checked into the Lion and Swan Hotel. After dressing for dinner, we went to the Lounge where we met an interesting bridal party. We then went to the dining room where we had French Cuisine. We met an interesting British retired Colonel and his wife. They were celebrating her birthday.

Friday, July12 we had another lovely breakfast in the bar area of the Lion and Swan. We left about 9:30 a.m. for Styal to tour THE QUARRY BANK MILL. We met Anne Roscoe, the P.R. person. She showed us the knitting room, the mill and museum. We purchased some cup-towels, aprons, etc. in the museum. This was very interesting as we could imagine what the original mill workers life was like. They lived in small company houses; purchased their food from the company store, and never got out of debt to the company. We were very happy we did not live during those times. I made a lot of photographs so I could show them to my students at R.H.S. We progressed on, arriving at Miller Howe Hotel in Windermere about 4 p.m. It was rainy and cool. We met the other two cars of girls in the lounge and then in to dinner at 8:30. We finished about 10:30 and went for a short walk, then to bed. Dinners at Windermere are a "work of art".

Saturday, July 13 we awakened to having coffee and a newspaper being delivered to our room. Our room was on the third floor and overlooked Lake Windermere. We had heated towel racks, plush white robes, a CD player, etc. In other words, it was wonderful. We had breakfast in the dining room at 9 a.m. We drove to Newly Bridge (small town) to look at antiques. We drove on to Ulverston to visit the Cumbria Crystal factory store. We purchased a few small vases, etc. to bring back for gifts. We drove on to Coniston where we saw children in costume for a "Sports Parade". We visited Henry Wordsworth Longfellows home, "Rydal Mount". It was in an Idyllic setting for writing. We got to see his desk where he composed much of his poetry. We returned to Miller Howe to rest a bit before dinner. Susan White , a home economics teacher in Garland and I got to visit the kitchens where we met Bill Tully the pastry chef and John Tovey, the head chef. I made photographs to share with my students. We had a wonderful dinner in the hotel dining room.

Sunday, July 14 after a great breakfast, we checked out of Miller Howe. We filled up with petrol—34.6 liters costing 16 pounds. We went to Levens Hall to see The Topiary Gardens. They were magnificent. We also toured the house. The couple who lived there with their two young sons, greeted us and then we toured the home which was lovely. We drove on to Hall House Farm to see the historic collection of farm implements and other things such as a restored calliope. We met the owners Olive and David Cheeseman. We still exchange Christmas letters each year. They were a lovely couple. We drove on to the Yorkshire Dales. We photographed the Wensleydale Heifer Hotel (described in James Herriott books) and drove on to Thirsk and had tea and scones at the Golden Fleece Hotel. We then drove to Kilburn because Glenie's maiden name was Kilburn. We saw blue roses in a garden there. We drove on to Richmond and checked into The Kings Head Hotel, room 14. We had a good nights rest.

Monday, July 15, we had a good breakfast at our hotel. We drove to York arriving about 11am. When we were walking to the Yorkminster, we stopped by the restaurant where Robert Thompson had carved a tiny mouse on the main door. This was his trademark he left on each of his carvings. I made a photograph of the mouse because I had read about Thompson using the mouse as his trademark on his carvings. We went to the Undercroft of Yorkminster to see the silver collection. We had a nice lunch in the Shambles area of York. We headed for Chelmorton and the Farmhouse we had reserved. The house had only one bath for six people. V.J.Beaty, of McKinney, TX. and Betty Clark of Waco shared the farmhouse with Glenie & Jim Byron and Joe and me. That was not too convenient. We drove into Buxton for dinner at Cheshire Cheese Pub. We had a nice visit with the chef. The food was very good. We got back to the farm, bathed and got to bed at eleven p.m.

Tuesday, July 16, we awakened about 7:00a.m., dressed and had a good breakfast which included boiled eggs, bacon, strawberries, toast and coffee. We drove into the town of Buxton and saw the Crescent,

(Caroline Rose Hunt patterned her Crescent Office Building in Dallas after this building), the Botanical Gardens, and had coffee at St. Ann's Hotel. The men walked up to the Palace Hotel while we shopped. We left Buxton about 1p.m. and arrived in Bakewell for a 1:30 lunch at Rutland Arms Hotel Lounge. Afterward, we visited a few antique shops. We just had to sample the famous "Bakewell Original Pudding" at Bloomies. We left there about 3p.m. and got to Haddon Hall in time for the last tour. The Byrons and Jurlinas headed for Chesterfield where we had a most wonderful dinner with Mary and Alvaro. Alvaro was Glenie's hairdresser, Alberto's brother. We drove back to the farm arriving about 10:30 p.m.

Wednesday, July 17, we left the farm and drove directly to Bakewell as we wanted to visit more antique stores. I went to Sinclair's China shop and bought some Toby mugs for Jason and Mike. We went to another part of Bakewell and I bought an Italian made, very colorful, tall vase at a thrift shop for Carol Ann. We arrived at Hardwick Hall about 1:30 p.m. It is a gorgeous place with rather plain gardens. We had sandwiches, tea, scones and strawberry flan in the tea room. We left at 3:30 p.m. headed for Derby (pronounced DARBY) to visit Denby Potteries. The factory store was closed so we went on to Sudbury. It is an ancient market place and is also the birthplace of Thomas Gainesborough (1727-88). There are several attractive medieval and 18th century houses. We went back to Buxton and had refreshment in the bar and dinner in the grill. It started to rain on us on the way back to the farm. We arrived about 10:30 p.m.

Thursday, July 18, was Jim's birthday (number 68). We sang Happy Birthday to Jim at breakfast. We drove to Matlock Bath to the Denby seconds store. I ordered 12 place settings of Daphne pattern (sweet peas) along with all the serving pieces. All of it cost around $300.00 and would be shipped in 3 months. (It arrived and I love it.) We drove to Lincoln arriving about 1:15 p.m. We had lunch at the Trust House Forte Buttery. We went to see the Lincoln Cathedral which is HUGE. The building was started in the year 1072 and is Gothic style. The Treasury contains the cathedral's original of Magna Carta and the foundation charter of William the Conqueror. It also has a changing collection of silver and gold appointments which are used in church services. We left the Cathedral about 4 p.m. and went to the Cheshire

Cheese Pub to celebrate Jim's Birthday. After dinner we went back to the farm and got to bed about midnight.

Friday, July 19, we headed to Stokesay to see and walk across the famed IRON BRIDGE which spans the Severn River. The small town was cute and we bought a couple of souvenirs at Bridge Street Bookshop. We stopped in a small cafe and had a cheese and onion sandwich and apple bread pudding for lunch. We drove on to Jackfield Tile Museum. We saw lovely tiles and huge pictures made of tiles. It was very interesting. We left there at 4:30 p.m. and drove to Coalport Museum and kiln. The displays of their discontinued figurines and other china pieces were beautiful. We drove back to Buxton for dinner at St. Anne's Hotel Grill. We drove back to the farm and packed so we could get an early start in the morning.

Saturday, July 20, we left Chelmorton Farm at Townend headed for Brierly Hill to visit the Royal Brierly Crystal factory and store. Of course we had to buy a few small pieces as gifts. We drove on to Coventry to visit what was left of the cathedral after WWII and the New Cathedral. Both left their impression on us. We had lunch at Warwick Castle and left for Chipping Campden. We checked into the King's Arms Hotel, walked around the town and up to St. James Church. We met the Byron's in the dining room for dinner. Took another short walk, bathed and washed my hair and went to bed.

Sunday, July 21, we got up at 6:30 a.m. to have breakfast and get to St. James church by 8 a.m. As in so many of the ancient churches, a huge cemetery is on the church grounds. Chipping Campden is such a beautiful area. They have used their cream colored stone in so many of their buildings and they are lovely. We packed and left at 10:30 headed for Sudeley Castle in Winchcombe. After touring the castle, we went to Glouscester. We had lunch at Chaucer's on Hare Lane at Northgate. We went to the cathedral for evening prayer. The vaulting in the Cloisters was beautiful. We had tea and shortbread in the Chapter House. At 4:30 p.m. we left for Monmouth via Ross on Wye on highway A-40. As we got into Wales, we saw Goodrich Castle Ruins. About 6:40 p.m. we arrived at Crown at Whitebrook Hotel. We had a glass of wine in the lounge and then went to the dining room for French Cuisine dinner. We got to bed about 10:30 p.m.

Monday, July 22, we woke up to rain. We drove to Tintern Abbey where it was raining even harder so we bought some slides rather than trying to make them. We drove on to Cardiff where we walked in light rain to tour the castle. Joe had a terrible cold and I was afraid he would take pneumonia, but he didn't. We encountered high winds and had to make detours to get back to our hotel - Old Ship in Mere.

Tuesday, July 23, it was sunny thank goodness. We had a lovely breakfast in our hotel and packed to leave Mere, England by 9:15 a.m. We drove to Stourhead to see the gardens. In 1741, Henry Hoare (a French gardener) was the first to create such a "freedom of nature" garden. With the help of Henry Flitcroft, an architect, they transformed a bare valley into a magnificent landscape dotted with small lakes, temples and grottoes. Color and variety has been the keynote. We progressed to the outskirts of Salisbury to visit "Wilton House", home of the Earls of Pembroke. Much of the architecture and decorative work were done by Indigo Jones in 1647 to reconstruct the part of the house which had been destroyed by fire. John Webb, Jones assistant, completed the work after Jones died in 1652. The home had beautiful artwork everywhere. We left there about 1 p.m. and headed for Petworth. We had tea and scones in the dining room. The house was not much to see compared to the others we had seen. We went on to Royal Tunbridge Wells in the Kent area. We visited a second hand bookstore and an antique store. We traveled on to the Kennil Holt Hotel. Joe and I had the Master Suite Room #6. It was large, had a queen-size bed, and was very comfortable. The ceiling had beautiful, large timbers across it. We had a lovely dinner in the dining room. Joe has developed a terrible sore throat and his cold isn't any better.

Wednesday, July 24, after a lovely breakfast, we walked around the premises and admired the huge gardens. The flowers were beautiful. We drove to Cranbrook where JoAnn and VJ went to a beauty shop to get their hair done. We stopped in Tinterden and bought lace runners at Mr. Leonard's Linen Shop. It was a huge shop with only linens for sale. We went on to see Scotney Castle Ruins and the gardens surrounding it. The castle was built in 1379. The gardens and pond were beautiful. We left there and had lunch at Happy Eater Restaurant about 2:30 p.m. We progressed to Sissinghurst Gardens which were simply beautiful the way they were laid out. We had an ice cream cone to cool off. We arrived back at Kennil Holt about 6 p.m., rested, bathed and dressed for dinner. The Byrons had invited Arthur and Kathleen Hall and Jessica and Sam Youd to come have dinner with us. The hotel served birthday cake for Jim Byron and Jerry Flowers (of Waco). After dinner, we had coffee in the Oak Room Lounge. At 10 p.m. Joe and I excused ourselves and went upstairs to pack because we leave for the airport and home in the morning.

Thursday, July 25, after a nice breakfast, Joe bought me a keepsake—a small box with Kennil Holt Hotel painted on the top. It is beautiful and a lovely keepsake. We drove to Gatwick, turned in our cars and checked in at American Airline about 10:30. Our plane took off promptly at 1:30 p.m. We arrived home 9 hours later at 6:30 p.m. our time. Carol Ann and Katherine met us and brought us home. Carol Ann kept our yard so nice while we were gone. She also got us a lovely bouquet of flowers and had a "Welcome Home" note by the arrangement. She even had purchased milk, bread, fruit, ground meat and cookies for us. What a sweetheart! After a bite to eat and a bath, we were ready for bed and sweet dreams about our lovely trip.

Appendix E:
Retirement Trip to Nova Scotia with Griffins- September 1987

Before I knew it, I was retiring on February 1st, 1987. Joe retired in August of 1987 and we bought a NEW suburban; talked Lee and Sylvia Griffin into accompanying us on a three week vacation to Nova Scotia and left September 6th. After our trip together 39 years ago we were looking forward to a fun time together again. We drove to Little Rock, Ark. the first day and spent the night at a Day's End.

Monday, September 7, we saw two 18-wheelers overturned on the way to Memphis. We had lunch at the Cotton Patch restaurant. We arrived in Elizabethtown, Ky. About 6p.m., checked in at Days Inn and had dinner at The Western Steer.

Tuesday, September 8, we left Elizabethtown after a good breakfast. At noon we arrived at The College Football Hall of Fame near Kings Head Island, Ky. That was quite interesting. After touring the building, we went to the largest and nicest McDonalds I have ever seen. It was cool and lovely so we sat on their huge patio to eat. At 5:30 p.m. we arrived at Dale and Betty Longs home. They lived on Beaver Bay Road near a lovely lake. They had a huge garden with all kinds of fresh vegetables growing and producing. Betty and Dale's daughter and family had been parishioners of Lees in Corpus Christi, Texas. (Lee was a Methodist minister) (Betty now lives with her daughter- now a Methodist minister in Smithville, TX.)

Wednesday, September 9, after a huge country breakfast with the Longs, we left about 9 a.m. and drove to Syracuse, N. Y. We got rooms for the night; then had dinner at Friendly's restaurant. About 8 p.m. the fire alarm went off and we had to change rooms. We had a good nights rest after that episode.

Thursday, September 10, we had a good breakfast and then drove to Rome, N. Y. We visited St. Peters Catholic Church and Zion Episcopal Church. They were both lovely. We went on to Erie Canal Village and toured all of the buildings and saw a boat being pulled up the canal by horses on shore beside the canal. (As an aside, Mike sent us a lovely black and white 2ft. x 6ft. drawing of Erie Canal when he was stationed in Germany. When it arrived, I was looking for some art work of

German buildings—not something from the U.S.) Seeing the village was very interesting. We arrived at Ed and Doris Mooridians in Troy, N.Y. about 4:30 p.m. Ed was one of Joe's good Army buddies back in 1944 & 1945. Ed and Doris drove us around their town. We saw where their daughter, Amy, went to high school; their furniture stores; and then they took us to dinner at the Troy Club. We went back to their home for coffee and dessert and got to bed about 11:30. Their home is large and lovely. Of course nothing would do but we all spend the night with them.

Friday, September11, we had a wonderful breakfast with Ed and Doris, looked over their lovely grounds and got on the road about 9:15. We drove most of the day and arrived at Round Pond, Maine about 5:30 p.m. Wintie Templeton, a former parishioner of Lees when he was in San Angelo lived there near her mother. Wintie's home is a white clapboard two story and has big lovely rooms. She welcomed the four of us with open arms.

Saturday, September 11, Sylvia and I got appointments at Mr. Louie's Corral Beauty Shop to get our hair washed and set. That worked out well. We shopped a little in downtown Damarascotta. We returned to Winties for coffee and fresh baked coffeecake. Her daughter, Madolyn, was there and we had a nice visit with her. We rode over to Round Pond and took a picnic lunch and ate on Wintie's mother's (Mrs. Hanna) beautiful terrace. The terrace overlooked the water. We then drove over to Pemaquid Point to see the lighthouse, the Atlantic Ocean, etc. It was so beautiful! We returned to Wenties and got ready to go to Boothbay Harbour. We saw the one-man submarine used by a Florida Research ship. We had dinner at Fisherman's Wharf, walked around and purchased some little gifts before returning to Round Pond and bed.

Sunday, September 13, we were up early, prepared a picnic lunch for the road. We went to 9 a.m. church (Methodist) with Wentie. Then, we went to Mrs Hannas with a group of church people for breakfast. We left at 11 a.m. for our trip to Nova Scotia via way of Bar Harbor, Maine. About 2p.m. we stopped in Ellsworth at Thomas Bay Picnic Grounds and ate the picnic lunch we had prepared earlier. We arrived in Bar Harbor about 3p.m. and checked into the Wonderview motel ($57.50). We picked up our ferry ticket ($63.20) and then drove up to the summit of Cadillac Mountain. It was foggy and rainy so we didn't get to see the lovely view we had hoped to see. This is the highest point on the Eastern U.S. Coast. We had dinner at the Moorings Restaurant ($l0.33). We returned to the motel and watched TV until bedtime.

Monday, September 14, we left the motel at 6:15 to get in line (we were the 7th vehicle in line) to make sure we got on the ferry. We had breakfast in the ferry dining room after Billie nursed an angina attack. The ride on the ferry was smooth, but we couldn't see anything because it was misty and cloudy. To pass the time(about 8 hours), we worked crossword puzzles, lost quarters to the one arm bandits, made photographs and visited the gift shop. We had lunch in the snack bar. We left the ferry at 3:30 p.m. and drove to the Tourism Center. That is a great thing. They ask the direction you plan to travel and let you look at a catalog of homes and farms that have rooms to let. You make a choice and they call and make reservations for you. We chose to spend the night at Whittaker Farm, arriving at 4:45p.m. For a lovely bedroom and shared bath, we paid $25.00. We had a lovely dinner at the Austrian Inn ($20.00).

Tuesday, September 15, the Whittakers prepared quite a breakfast for us. We had fresh fruit cocktail, cooked cereal, bacon, eggs, apple juice, toast or muffin and coffee. Mrs Whittaker had taught school 30 years. We asked the Whittakers about their winters. They said sometimes the snow reached the top of their first floor windows so they left the farm with their son and spent the winter in Florida. That gave us a chuckle. We walked around the farm, made photos of the animals and left at 9a.m. We traveled down Route 1 on the Evangeline Trail. We stopped at St. Mary's Catholic church at ll:50 a.m. It is beautiful and the largest wooden structure in North America. We saw another lovely church, St. Bernard's. We arrived at Digby and ate a picnic lunch on a bench overlooking the cove. We drove off leaving my purse with all our travelers checks under the bench. Several miles out of town I realized I didn't have my purse so we drove back and it was still under the bench—THANKS BE TO GOD! We were on the road again at 2:50p.m. We saw our first Methodist Church in the outskirts of Digby, but it is a museum. We were on our way to Port Royal. At exit 23 we stopped to locate our way when Stephen Outhouse, a woodcarver, stopped to offer help. We followed him into Annapolis Royal Museum. In Aylesford, we had rooms at THE DOCTOR"S Bed & Breakfast. It was a big two story white wooden home. The Dr. had had his offices on the west side of the home. Brad & Ingrid Haworth made the offices into a museum of sorts. Their huge barn housed an antique shop. Joe and I had the maid's quarters as our room ($35.00). There was a steep stairway from the room down to the kitchen. We had a private bath. It was lovely. We had dinner at Helen's restaurant ($17.80).

Wednesday, September 16, we had a lovely breakfast of hot muffins, eggs, juice and coffee. I bought a small antique oblong bowl (they were using it as a soap dish in our bathroom) for $16.50. The design in the bottom of the dish is an English Abbey (in blue) which we saw when we were in England. We went to Kentville to visit Sylvia's cousin. We then went to Halls Harbor to watch the tide going out at channel Minas. We stopped in Wolfville for lunch at the Colonial Inn Restaurant ($12.00). The Acadian College is located here. We went to the Grand Pree' sandy beach and saw the Grand Pree' Community Church which was erected in 1861. A statue of Evangeline was down the sidewalk about 100 ft. in front of the church. We went to the tourist bureau and were asked if we were from Texas— and told us we had a call and we should call Sylvia's cousin. We called her and she said Mike had called for Joe. He wanted to wish Dad a Happy Birthday. We drove on to Windsor, got a room at Hampshire Court House ($42.00). We drove out to see the "BORE", but when the tide came in it rolled in very slow and did not form a large bore like we had hoped it would. We returned to our room which was upstairs with a private bath. It rained during the night and was still raining when we woke up on Thursday.

Thursday, September 17, we left the hotel, drove a while and then stopped for breakfast at Motel Downsview. Several miles down the highway, we stopped to photograph St. Peter's Anglican Church which is near Peggy's Cove. The sun had come out by the time we got to Peggy's Cove. The lighthouse was very picturesque. It is built on solid rock. We ate lunch at Peggy's Cove ($16.50). We made many pictures there. A lot of Joe's slides turned out to be very light. We stopped in Dover to photograph a red boat dry-docked on an island. It was very pretty. We drove on to Halifax. It is quite a large town. We walked through the Citadel and some historic properties. We walked down to the water and saw the famous Bluenose II sailing vessel. We had a root beer and some shortbread at the wharf. We sat at a picnic table on benches. On a lighter note, Lee turned his bench over backward and landed on the sidewalk. Thank goodness he wasn't hurt. We drove on to Bible Hill where we had rooms at Eleanor's Bed and Breakfast. After a light dinner downtown, we drove out to Truro to see another BORE. When the tide came in, it was just a lazy ripple—no BORE. Back to the B&B and to bed.

Friday, September 18, we had a lovely breakfast. Lee surprised us by saying he had to see a dentist. He thought he had an abscessed tooth. Our host called their dentist, Dr. Johnson, and he gave Lee a shot of penicillin and some pain pills. We left about 12:15 and stopped at Heather motel for lunch ($15.75) at the edge of New Glasgow. We got on the Cabot Trail at 4:15 p.m. We bought some souvenir coins at the travel bureau. We had reservations at The Roost where we checked in about 6p.m.($30.00). The Roost was 2.3 miles south of highway 105 in Big Harbor, Baddeck, Nova Scotia. It was owned by Mrs. Lil Coleman, wife of a deceased dentist. Another couple stayed at the Roost who were from Wooster, Mass. He was a judge. We went back to the Bell Museum for a film at 7:15 p.m. The museum was lovely. It had everything related to the invention of the telephone.

Saturday, September 19, we sang Happy Birthday to Joe at breakfast. I had told Lil the night before that it was Joe's birthday so she pulled out all the stops. She used her fine china, crystal and silver and served a three-course breakfast. We used her binoculars to look across the lake and see Mr. Bell's home. We left The Roost about 9:45 and stopped at Harbor Rest Lighthouse. We stopped in Chetticamp for lunch ($17.83). We stopped at Keltic Lodge, a huge hotel, and had refreshments. We reached Antigonish and checked into the Colonial Inn Motel ($47.00). We had birthday dinner at the Moonlight restaurant. We saw a couple of policemen so I asked them to drive by our motel often to keep an eye on our Texas SUV. One of them said "if it's from Texas, it's so big no one could run off with it. (The motel was pretty ratty—not like a home B&B)

Sunday, September 20, we drove to Glasgow for breakfast at Smitty's ($15.80). We took the ferry over to Prince Edward Island. It cost $10.40 per person. Upon arrival at Charlottetown, we took a tour bus around the city. It was very warm, but we enjoyed seeing the town. After the tour, we went in the Bascillica of St. Dunstan's. We drove out to see Green Gables, the house used as the backdrop for Maude

Montgomery's book "Anne of Green Gables". We toured the house which was lovely and just as Maude described it in her story. We arrived at The Blue Heron B&B where we had reserved rooms ($30.00). The home was owned by Mr. and Mrs. Milton Weeks. The home was located on Stanley Bridge River. We drove to Chez Yvonne Restaurant for dinner ($26.37). We drove back to the B&B and Adelaide showed us around the house. It was new and lovely. Joe and I had the master suite w/private bath. It overlooked the lake.

Monday, September 21, we went for a walk before breakfast. The Weeks dog went with us. Upon returning from our walk, we had a lovely breakfast with another guest from Tennessee. The preserves were made by Aidelaide of Rhubarb, pineapple, oranges and a "speck" of lemon. We were on the road by 9 a.m. We stopped at Woodleigh to get a "Glimpse of Britain". The buildings are miniatures of many of the famous English buildings such as St. Paul's Cathedral. Most are tall enough for people to walk through. We left there about 10:40, arriving for the ferry to Cape Tormentine, N. B. at ll:l5 a.m. ($7.60 per couple). We arrived at Moncton in time for lunch at Cy's Seafood ($24.53). The restaurant was lovely and the food was delicious. We drove to St. Andrew's by the Sea and got a room at the Picket Fence Motel ($49.95). We had dinner at Smuggler's Wharf ($16.00).

Tuesday, September 22, we left the motel and drove to Calais and had breakfast at the Airline Restaurant ($8.00). As we crossed the river into Bangor, Maine, I photographed a beautiful church steeple. We stopped at a laundramat to wash our dirty belongings. Joe and Lee left Sylvia and me there while they went to wash the Suburban. We were back on the road by 11 a.m. We stopped in Augusta, Maine for a late lunch at Howard Johnson's ($10.80). We arrived back at Winties about 3 p.m. She prepared a wonderful dinner for us: pork roast, mashed potatoes, peas, gravy, sliced tomatoes, butterscotch pie and ginger squares. After dinner we drove with Wintie to New Harbor to hear her church bell choir practice.

Wednesday, September 23, we all slept late, had a good breakfast and dressed for the day. Wintie was a real estate sales person and she left to take care of a deal. Our guys left to make photographs. Wintie returned about 10:30 and we fixed a light lunch and ate when our guys returned. Wintie took Sylvia and me for a ride to Pemmiquid Point around the cove. We saw Fort William Henry. We stopped at an antique place to look and shop. I bought an etched glass toothpick holder. That evening we took Wintie and her mother (Mrs. Hanna) to dinner at Gosnold Arms Inn Restaurant. The seafood was great and so was the atmosphere. On the way back, we stopped to see Jeff's house he had built and was still working on. (Jeff is Wintie's youngest son.) We returned to the farm and went to bed promptly as we were tired.

Thursday, September 24, we left Winties about 9 a.m. after a huge breakfast. We stopped in Freeport to see all of the outlet stores. L.L. Bean was something to see just because of it's size. Joe bought a nice weatherproof red jacket at London Fog outlet. We drove on to Kennebunkport where we saw the Wedding Cake House. We had a picnic lunch on the grounds of the Franciscan Monastery in a covered pavilion overlooking the body of water across from President Bush's property. Back on the road—stopped on the Massachusetts turnpike for R & R and gasoline—then continued on IS84 to Southington, Conn. We spent the night at a Comfort Inn ($49.00). We had dinner at Denny's ($7.71).

Friday, September 25, we drove to Danbury, Conn. for breakfast at "Friendly's" ($8.20). We got on Ticonic Parkway and exited at exit 16 to make photos of the Hudson River. We got on the New Jersey Turnpike and exited at exit 40 for lunch at Roy Rogers ($9.06). We left the N.J. turnpike, crossed the Deleware River Bridge about 2:30 p.m. and at 4:30 we stopped at Howard Johnsons for refreshments. We were at the corner of Maryland. We drove on to Pocomo, Va. and entered the toll for Chesapeake Bay Bridge. The sun was almost setting as we drove across the bay. We got some fabulous photographs. Lee and Sylvia knew a young lady (Lynette) who lived in Norfolk with her two children (Emily and Jesse) while her husband served in the navy. We spent the night with them.

Saturday, September 26, we saw Lynette off to work and we went to Denny's for breakfast. We crossed the tunnel at 10 a.m. on Highway 64 on our way to Old Colonial Williamsburg, Va. We had lunch at Chowning's Tavern. We enjoyed seeing Bruton Parish and all of the little shops. We got a room at Red Roof Inn ($39.00) and had dinner at the Holiday Inn across the street. It was not very good.

Sunday, September 27, we had breakfast at Hardee's next door ($3.86). We stopped in St. Petersburg and saw St. Peters Episcopal Church which was beautiful. We got on highway 85 and went to South Hill, Va. We attended church at All Saints Episcopal and the rector was Susan Bowman. We had lunch at a Golden Corral ($11.95). We stopped in Greensboro, N. C. for R&R. We went to Kannapolis to Cannon Village (a discount village). I bought a dress at the Manhattan Shop. We drove on to Charlotte where we spent the night at another Red Roof Inn.

Monday, September 28, HAPPY BIRTHDAY to ME!!! (Age 63). We were up early and walked over to Shoney's for breakfast ($9.20). We drove a couple of hours and stopped at a Cracker Barrel in Greenville, N.C. for R&R. Sylvia bought and gave me an embroidered piece that said "Friends are Life's Most Precious Treasures". We stopped in Atlanta for lunch at a Dairy Queen just after I.S. 20 entrance. It was not very good. We changed time zones and gained an hour. About 3:40 we stopped in Bessimer, MS. For refreshments at a Shoney's. We spent the night at Meridian, Ms. at a Day's Inn ($36.89).

Tuesday, September 29, we awakened refreshed and had breakfast at The Country Restaurant ($8.74). We drove to Vicksburg and went by to see Betty and Cliff Whitney at their Bed and Breakfast. Betty had worked as a Counselor at Richardson High School so we enjoyed seeing them. We had lunch in Monroe, La. and drove on in to Richardson late that afternoon. The trip was a lovely experience. I forgot to mention the leaves were turning red and gold in Maine and the north as we made our return trip.

We experienced our first trip with Lee and Sylvia to Yellowstone and 40 years later we were able to experience this trip to Nova Scotia with them. GOD is GOOD!!! and FRIENDS are WONDERFUL.

Appendix F:
Diary of Trip to Croatia

In 2001, Mike and his family and Joe and I left June 24 from DFW on a 777 airliner for Zurich, Switzerland. We had a 4 hour wait before flying on to Zagreb, Croatia so we toured the airport. It is a small city within the airport with all kinds of beautiful shops. We boarded a small Swiss Air plane to Zagreb. We were like sardines in a can. Nikola (Nick) Jurlina, son of Mira and Milan Jurlina of Vancouver, and two of his college friends met us at the airport in Zagreb. We got our rental van and followed them into Zagreb and checked into our hotel, the Sheraton. It was a lovely hotel and their food was wonderful. Nick and his brother, Hrvoje (Hrv), met us in the lobby and visited about an hour. They were having college finals so they left to study with the assurance they would meet us the next day. That evening our family walked to the GUSTEK restaurant, just a few blocks from the hotel to have dinner. Robert, our waiter was very pleasant as were the surroundings in the restaurant. Just as we finished ordering our meal, the electricity went off. No food could be cooked so we ordered wine, cheese, fruit and wonderful breads. It was a nice experience. We walked to the railway station (Kolodvor) and back past a park to our hotel and to bed. It was a long day.

Tuesday, June 26 Joe and Nick went to the University Library where the Archives of Croatia are stored. They explained to the librarian what they were looking for and after some consternation on her part she said they would have to come back the next day as she needed time to get the microfilms they would need to look at. Later, Joe, Mike and family and I met Nick and Hrv and walked around town making pictures. As we walked in the huge city square, we came upon a puppeteer who made his small puppet play the piano (looked like it anyway). The puppet kept time with the music from a boombox. It was fascinating to watch and hear. We walked through a beautiful glass-domed building that turned out to be a shopping mall. We continued to walk around the Old Zagreb square as Hrv told us about the statue of King Tomislav mounted on his stallion which looked out over New Zagreb. While Croatia was under the control of the Serbian Communists the statue faced toward Serbia (east); however, since the Republic of Croatia has severed ties with Serbia, the statue now faces New Zagreb (south). We walked up 200 steps to the top of the old walled city where we saw St.

Mark's Catholic Church with its colorful tiled roof which proved to be the flag of Croatia. The church dates back to the 9th century. Leaving St. Marks we walked through an old gate that had the date 760 inscribed over the entrance. As we walked down the path into a sort of tunnel, we came upon a shrine where people pause to pray where a miracle of some kind took place many moons ago. Coming out of the tunnel, we passed a small green grassy area that contained a statue of St. George and the slain dragon. We stopped at a sidewalk café for refreshments as we were hot and thirsty. We walked up Skalenska Street to visit the Cathedral of St. Stephens. It dates back to the early days of Zagreb. It was a huge building and many works of the German artist, Albrecht Durer were on display. The outside of the cathedral was practically encased in metal framework as they were replacing the exterior stone one stone at the time. The original organ was still in use. After touring the Cathedral, we walked downhill to a Croatian Restaurant where we had a lovely dinner on the outdoor patio. The name was Restaurant Kapitolska. The food was great as was the company of our Croatian cousins. We walked back to the Sheraton and to bed.

Wednesday, 27 June Hrv and Nick came by the hotel for a brief visit before Joe and Nick returned to the Library to view the microfilms. Mike and family and I took the video camera and toured around the country outside Zagreb. We visited a castle and on leaving, we were going downhill the wrong way on a one-way street so we were stopped by two policemen. We followed them back to the castle, went to the restaurant and bought drinks for the very nice policemen.

Thursday, 28 June we drove to Novo Mesto and Ljubljana in Slovenia to look for records of Joe's maternal grandparents—the Telbans and Novaks but found no records. There was just not enough time to do actual research. We saw many beautiful churches and vineyards on the way to Nova Mesto. We stopped in downtown and had a cold drink under a huge umbrella in front of Dodo's pub. We walked through city hall and over to St. Leonard's Church. Unfortunately there didn't seem to be anyone to speak to about family records so we just enjoyed the scenery. We drove up a hillside to see The Church of St. Urban, constructed in 1620. We had a beautiful view of the vineyard covered hillsides and the valleys below. In a glass cubicle at the back of the church was a full size statue of St. Urban dressed in his clerical robes.

On the way back we stopped at a vineyard, Krkin Hram, which had been in business since 1917 and sampled wines. This winery had a beautiful outdoor patio under a grape arbor where they could cater large affairs. We bought three bottles of wine. We drove on forty miles to Ljubljana, the capital of Slovenia. We had lunch at Gostilna Sestica. Then we drove out to see the castle Ljubljana. It was big, interesting and Mike and his family walked up 163 steps to the top of the tower. I made a photo of them looking over the edge. We returned to Zagreb and to the Sheraton for our last night.

Friday, 29 June we checked out of the hotel after breakfast and drove south toward Seline and Zadar to visit Nick and Hrvs' mother, Mira. As we approached the community of Karlovac, we saw the first signs of the Croat-Serbian War of 1991 – 1993. Homes and buildings had been shot up and some had been burned out. War is so sad! Further down the road, a series of small buildings had been abandoned as a result of incendiary grenades/mortars. In the countryside, we saw electric lines that had been repaired by replacing destroyed poles with hand cut trees in order to get the lines back in service quickly. As we drove along, there would be a café or store just out in the middle of nowhere it seemed. Next to it would be a huge grill where they were grilling fowls or lambs. A few miles further, we came upon a totally destroyed café. Only the walls were standing. This was an attempt of the Serbs to destroy the morale of the people. We stopped and walked through this building. A man was painting a huge sign on the outside wall large enough to read from the highway. Meanwhile Jacob took the movie camera and was roaming the property. He came upon a live snake and moved away from it very fast. As we continued toward Seline, we got our first glimpse of an arm of the beautiful blue Adriatic Sea. Driving into Seline (small community), we wondered how to find Mira Jurlina. Then, we saw a sign ZIMMER JURLINA (meaning rooms) at a driveway. Mike turned in and we saw the four home compound we had been told about. The homes were all multistory. Mira and Milans home was about 75 feet from the Adriatic. It was a three story home with rooms to let. We stayed on the second floor as the third floor was still incomplete. Mira's husband and three sons have constructed this huge brick building. They shipped all of the bath fixtures and refrigerator and washing machine from Canada. They had two bedrooms with private baths on either side of a nice kitchen and sitting area that roomers could use. Mira prepared a lovely dinner which we ate out on the second floor balcony while watching the beautiful sunset over the Adriatic.

Saturday, June 30 after breakfast, our family plus Mira went to visit Cousin Ante "Bele" Jurlina. He is one of Joe's Uncle Sam's sons. He had recently returned from Germany after retiring as a tinsmith-mechanic to redo and live in his and Joe's grandfather's home. The older homes built around 1914 are similar to our townhouses. Four or five homes are located in one long stone building. This home is a short distance east and north and up the mountainside a few hundred yards from Mira's. We had to walk several yards to gain entrance to the property. Bele met us at the gate to his property dressed in white shorts and barefoot. He was 70 yrs old in 2001. He had recently recovered from a triple by-pass heart surgery but seemed very energetic. He showed us around the place including the "dilapidated" building where Joe's father was born. Only the stone walls and red tile roof were standing. The floor between the living quarters and the lower area where the animals stayed at night remained. Returning to his home, he showed us his kitchen, bath, and living room which he had recently remodeled. They were modern and attractive. On the patio he had three wooden three-legged stools that Joe's grandfather Joseph had made over a hundred years ago. We sat out on the patio drinking a glass of wine and conversing. Bele spoke mostly in German. Jacob had had two years of German at St. Marks School for Boys so he could interpret for us. Mira also helped with the interpreting. Bele agreed to come to Miras in the afternoon. We drove around the village of Selina and stopped at Villa Antica. The Hostel was owned by another of Joe's first cousins Ante Jurlina, the youngest son of Pop's sister, Antica. (Pop called her Anna). This lovely three story building had been heavily damaged by the Serbs. We met Ante at his brother Franks who lived next door to the hostel. The brothers with help from the Croatian government were planning to restore the hostel. The hostel consisted of small apartments and the basement was a wine cellar with big casks for the wine. After visiting these two cousins, Mira directed us to the Catholic Church Joe's father attended as a boy and served as an acolyte (pictures next page). He used to tell us stories about walking along the Adriatic and throwing stones into the sea on his way to church. The church is beautiful but probably would only seat about 50 to 60 people. While we were inside, Joe said "Oh, how I wish pop knew we were here"! Mira spoke up immediately and said, "He probably does". We

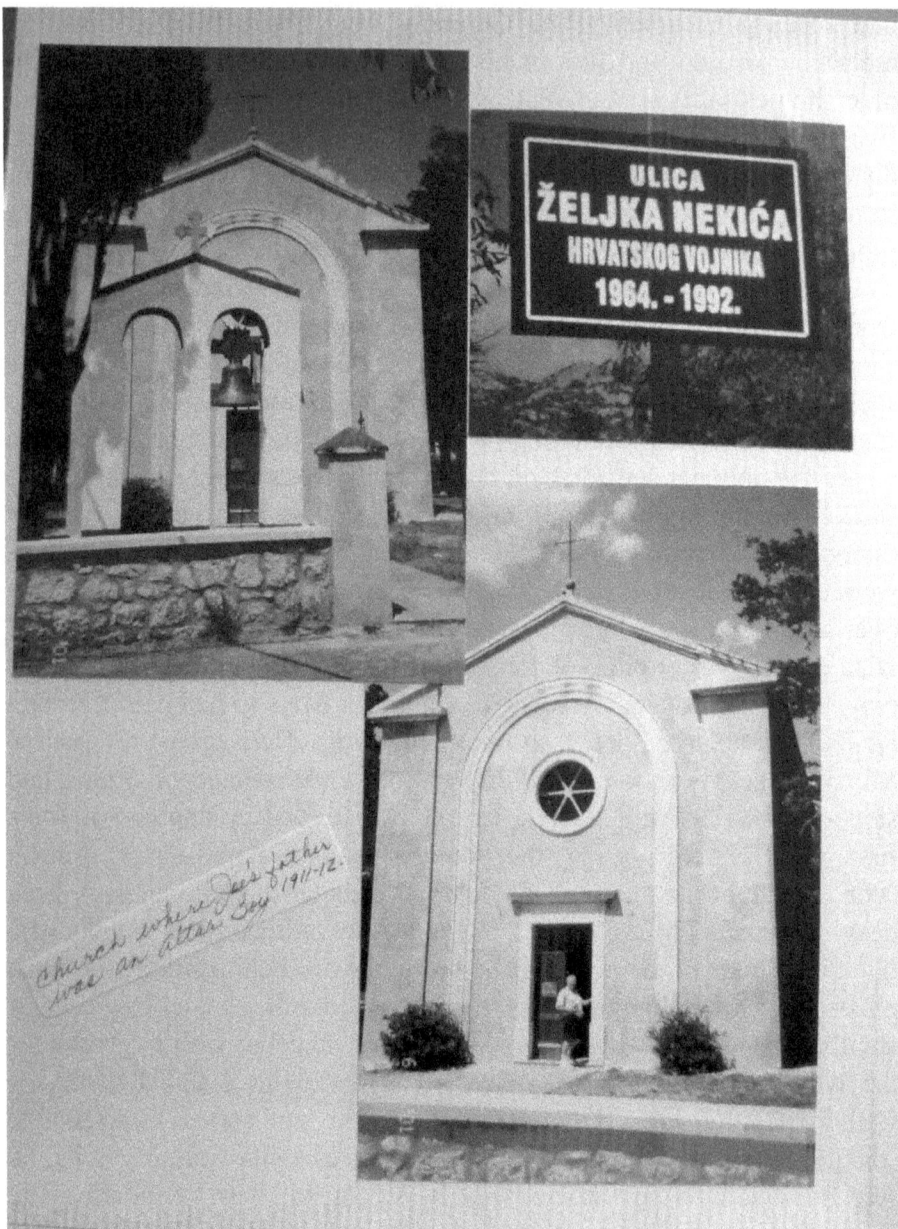

Church where Joe's father was an altar boy 1911-1912

had lunch at Miras and after Bele arrived, we drove to the "/Seline Cemetery. Most of the people who were buried there were Jurlinas. Most of the headstones had a Croatian phrase on them, "TIHI DOM OBITELJ JURLINA which roughly translated means "The last quiet home for the Jurlina family". Joe found some names and dates he needed, but did not find his great-great grandfather, Jacob's grave. He died after 1836. On the way back to Mira's, we visited Milan's parents who lived just across the driveway with their son Tome and wife Bozica. We had a lovely visit with Mira doing all the interpreting. Mira prepared octopus potato salad for dinner. It was one of the best meals we had on the trip and we enjoyed eating on

the second floor balcony again.

Sunday, July 1, after breakfast we walked around the beach looking out over the beautiful Adriatic where the grandchildren had fun wading, swimming and running around and taking a look at the Jurlina compound that we had called "home" for several days. Bele had invited the six of us plus Mira for Sunday lunch at his place. He brought out his portable grill, made a fire and picked fresh lettuce and tomatoes from his garden. He grilled pork steaks while Pam and Sabrina washed the veggies and made a great salad. We enjoyed seeing the beautiful grape vines loaded with small grapes hanging over the second floor banister. After lunch Bele proposed that Jacob should come back to Croatia and he would give him the home where Pop Jurlina had grown up prior to coming to the U. S. A. in 1913. After lunch and visiting, we bid Bele farewell and returned to Mira's for a short nap. Later in the day we drove up the coast a few miles to Starigrad-Paklenica to view some of the ruins of buildings destroyed by the Serbian army during the 1991-92 conflict. On our return, we stopped at the castle ruins that were visible from Mira's home. We then returned to Mira's so the children could take one last swim.

Monday, July 2 we drove up the coast about 4 miles to the Paklenica Park in the Velebit Mountains. We parked at the gate and walked up a narrow paved path and watched several climbers scaling the steep rock wall of the mountains on either side of the path. As we walked back toward the parking lot, we saw the door to Marshall Tito's war-room which was located deep within the mountain. Had we been there on a weekday, we could have toured the war room. Mira said the area could house a force of 200 or more personnel. We stopped at a small souvenir stand to purchase some postcards. On our return to Seline we stopped at St. Peter's Church and cemetery to watch archeologists digging on the property. Their digging had produced some jewelry items that they tagged and said they would be displayed in the Zagreb museum. The church dates back to the 9 or 10th century. We made our final return to Mira's, packed up our van and headed south toward Zadar after a tearful goodbye. We drove to Zadar to view the seacoast and the many marinas right downtown. There were hundreds of beautiful boats tied up. It is an old coastal town. Joe's cousin, Ante had lived there with his wife, son and two daughters. Soon after the war started, Mira sought political asylum in London. We and Mike and Pam visited her in London in 1990, but have not been able to maintain contact with her. Her parents divorced and her father went back to Seline which really disturbed her. Her sister, Anita and brother Marin took asylum in Italy. On leaving Zadar, and arriving in Plitvice, we stopped at a new and very modern restaurant for a bowl of goulash and ice cream for dessert. We went through the town of Slunj and crossed the Korana River several times. We stopped twice to observe the beautiful waterfalls. Arriving in Zagreb at the Sheraton, we had a late dinner in the dining room. Then to bed we went.

Tuesday, July 3 we invited Hrvoje and Nicholas Jurlina to have a farewell breakfast with us at our hotel. Then we headed for the airport, checked in our Ford Transit van and boarded our flight to Zurich, Switzerland. We had a two hour layover in Zurich before boarding a plane for Frankfurt, Germany. We spent the night at a hotel at the airport in Frankfurt.

Wednesday, July 4 we boarded an afternoon flight on a Boeing 767 arriving in Dallas on Wednesday a.m. On the flight to DFW we saw the movie "ANTITRUST". We also napped a lot. It was a wonderful trip, but it was also wonderful to be home.

Appendix G:
Diary of Trip to New Zealand

The six Jurlinas left home on July 7, 2004. Joe and I got to fly first class due to AAdvantage tickets. We met up with Mike and family in LAX airport and had dinner together. Our flight to Auckland was #26 and took 11 hours. Joe and I were on the third level in the plane. We had great leg room and the food was delicious. Our plane was a 747-4 and holds 430 people. It was full too. Joe and I deplaned first and made a photo of the young Jurlinas as they deplaned. We went through customs and got our rental van and drove to the Holiday Inn Centra where we had reservations.

It is now July 9th. Time flys when you cross the ocean. HA! At 3:30 this afternoon, we visited the War Memorial Museum that was built in 1929. It is beautiful and has artifacts from each war since that date. We drove to downtown Auckland for dinner at the base of the Sky Tower. After dinner, we went up to the top of the tower and walked around the observations floor. The night view of Auckland is beautiful. This tower is the tallest in the world. Back to the hotel and to bed for we were all exhausted.

Saturday, July 10th Sabrina and I slept until 9 a.m. Joe and Mike went to a neighborhood store and got rolls, juice and fruit for breakfast. We left the motel about 10:30 and drove up to the Obelisk. On the way up the hill, we passed a beautiful farm with pretty cattle and sheep. We had a great view of downtown Auckland from there. We drove into Auckland and walked around the waterfront. We had on our winter coats and were happy to have them. The wind blowing off the water was COLD. We had lunch at "Café on the Water". It was very good. We then walked down the street to a nice mall. Pam bought two or three knit caps as gifts. They represented the New Zealanders "ALL BLACK RUGBY TEAM". I bought Carol Ann a silver and Abalone drop necklace. (I hope she likes it.) Mike and family went to the Rugby Game tonight while Joe and I watched it on TV. It is an exciting game.

Sunday, July 11 we had made contact with Cousin Ivan Jurlina and were invited to their farm home for Sunday lunch. We checked out of our hotel and drove to Kaitai and arrived at Ivan's farm about 12:15.

Ivan and Mary have two sons and three daughters. One daughter lives in Australia, but the other family members were present. Ivan's brother Boris, his wife and three children were there too. After lunch, Ivan, Joe and Boris had much conversation and compared notes trying to see exactly how they are related. Ivan's son Michael and our Michael drove into town and got us adjoining rooms at the Taipa Bay Resort. The teenagers took Sabrina and Jacob to see a movie. The theatre was an old Croatian Hall with a large home screen. They warned Sabrina and Jacob not to speak or the lady in charge would charge them more as they were foreigners. They brought Sabrina and Jacob to our hotel after the movie. We were preparing for bed when the phone rang. It was Michael saying they had had a family discussion and wanted us to come back Tuesday afternoon to see his and Lisa's home and David (his brother) wanted Jacob and Sabrina to see the dairy cows (450) being milked. Ivan was planning to cook a lamb on his spit and all the women were bringing dishes of food so we readily accepted.

Monday, July 12 after breakfast at the hotel and a walk along the beach, we drove to Kaitaia and visited the Ancient Kauri Kingdom shop and café. We bought some souvenirs. A cataclysmic event occurred about 30 to 50,000 years ago that felled and covered up the Kauri forests. In the 1880s people in New Zealand discovered the trees under the earth and started digging them up. They used the wax on the roots to make varnish and linoleum and other products. They use the wood to make furniture and other wooden products to sell. We drove to Milan and Annette's home a few miles north of Kaitia. Milan and his brother, Victor showed us their father's "Sweetwater Museum".

They have hundreds of bags of the Kauri Gum. Some of the pieces of gum are very large and worth a lot of money. Annette showed us their home which is lovely. She let Sabrina play her piano and she remarked "those ivories have never been tickled like that before". Annette then invited the men in and provided tea, buttered scones, and cookies for lunch. We sat around their breakfast table and talked for 2 or 3 hours. We bid them goodbye and said we would see them on Wednesday morning. Victor had invited us back so he could take us on a tour of their property and the countryside nearby. We left and drove to Cooper's Beach area and had dinner at the Waterfront Café. We went back to the motel and the children went to bed. The adults played "Goin' Fishing" and "Poker Hands". We headed to bed at 10:30.

Tuesday, July 13 Mike and Pam prepared and served breakfast in their room. We sang HAPPY BIRTHDAY to Jacob as he is 17 today. We picked Victor up at 10 a.m. and he showed us an avocado orchard, his brother's cattle, 90 mile beach, and we ended up at a gum digger's park. That was interesting. They had huts like the gumdiggers lived in when they arrived in New Zealand from Croatia in the late 1800s. Inside the huts they had examples of the homemade beds they slept on, etc. We saw how they dug for the trees below the surface of the earth. Victor was an interesting conversationalist. He was a chemical engineer, but retired when Heinz bought out their company. He now works part time as a disc jockey. We returned to Milan's home a little after lunch where we met all 17 members of their family.

Milan's daughter has a daughter named Jurlina Carroll—Carroll being her last name. Most of the family members had driven up from Auckland. We were invited to stay for lunch but we declined and drove to the Ancient Kauri Kingdom and ate lunch at the café. We went to the bakery in Kaitai to pick up the birthday cake Pam had ordered to take to Ivan's for dinner. The cake was like a jelly roll covered with chocolate frosting and said "Happy Birthday Jacob" on top. It was about 30 inches long and about 5 inches high. We went by Mike and Lisa's home. They built on top of a hill just south of Ivan's place. It is a very nice place and certainly had a 360 degree view. We took the cake by Mary and Ivan's and drove on down the road to David and Nada's place. David thought the children would enjoy seeing the 400+ dairy cows being milked which they did. We visited the pens where the baby calves were kept and fed by bottle until old enough to wean. They were so pretty and I stuck my hand out to pet one and it started sucking my finger. It must have been really hungry. Pam and I went in Nada's house and helped her prepare a rice salad she would take to Mary's for dinner. Her house was new and they had a huge deck on the front. It was very nice. We got to Mary and Ivan's about 5:30 and he and Mike were cooking a lamb on a spit in the garage. Ivan had also cut up sweet potatoes and deep fried them. When the lamb was done, we watched Mike and David remove it from the spit and carve the meat. In addition to Ivan (71), and Mary, others in attendance included their three oldest children plus grandchildren:

Michael (43), Lisa (Vinac) (36), dtr. Darnelle (15) son Nicholas (12) lives on farm

David (41), Nada (Radojkovich) (39), Brandon (12) Mitchell (10) Haydon (8)

Sharon Jurlina (39) Russell Hilton Jonas, Emma (11) Daniel (10) Josh (8) lives in Auckland

Yvonne Jurlina (38) Hamish Buxton, Abby (5), Luke (3), Grace (1) lives in Auckland (not at the dinner)

Angela Jurlina (30) was not present and lives in Sydney, Australia

Boris (Ivan's brother) (72) and wife Jean Wooldridge

Boris, Jr. (19), Christopher (18), Elizabeth (16)

Betty (Ivan's sister) 68) and husband Joe Yukich

Joseph (79), Billie (79), Mike (52), Pam (53), Jacob (17), Sabrina (13)

This was quite a group of Jurlina relatives. The women brought several types of vegetable dishes and salads to go with the lamb and sweet potatoes. What a dinner! The children ate in the living room and the adults ate at the dining table. After dinner, the table was cleared and we asked the children to come around the dining table. Jacob was so surprised to see the birthday cake. Ivan said he couldn't remember his 17th birthday but he hoped Jacob would remember his and all the relatives who were there to wish him a HAPPY BIRTHDAY. Jacob thanked him and the entire family for their wonderful hospitality. David lit the big birthday candle and Boris led us in singing Happy Birthday. It was really almost indescribable the close feelings we developed in such a short time for all these relatives. (We still talk on the phone and send e-mails in 2008.) We returned to the hotel and to bed by 11 p.m.

Wednesday, July 14 Mike and family had planned to go on a fishing trip and were ready to go at 9 a.m., but the man that was to take them had to call it off due to rain and wind. We called Ivan, Mike, David, and Victor one more time to thank them for their hospitality and then we packed the car and headed toward Rotorua, N. Z. It is a holiday town, but wouldn't you know the rain got worse as we drove north and then west. We saw such beautiful scenery: mountains, valleys, forests, and even saw sand dunes next to the Tasmian Sea. Mike and family walked down to the sea, but it was so windy Joe and I stayed in the car. We had to take a ferry across to Rowenta and observed a beautiful rainbow on the way. By now it was 4 p.m. and we were starving. We finally found a small café that made hamburgers for us and we had ice cream for dessert. Continuing on our way, we drove through a Kouri tree forest. They were 20 to 30 feet in diameter. I couldn't tell you how tall they were. We arrived in Dargaville about 7:30 p.m. We got rooms at the Parkview Motel, unloaded the car and went to eat at "The Steak House". The owner had the employees leave the outside door open so take-out customers could get their orders. We almost froze. As we left, I asked to speak to the manager. I told him if he would come to Texas, we would be more hospitable.

Thursday, July 15 we got up at 7 a. m., showered and dressed while Mike went to the grocery store. When he returned, he and Pam made breakfast. We got on the road about 10 a. m. When we arrived in Paparoa, Dad spotted a bowling lawn club which was under water from the rain of last night. We drove on to Matakobid and went to a larger Kouri museum. It was much larger than the one in Kaitaia. We had lunch at a café called "The Coffee Hut". It was at a crossroads on the highway—no town around. We drove on to Kameu and realized we were going the wrong direction. As we were turning around, we saw Gladys Jurlina Oliver running toward us. We had met her at Milan and Victor's home on Monday. She said she and her husband had passed us on the highway, turned around and came back to talk to us. (Gladys is Milan and Victor's sister.) They guided us to the Kumau River Winery where we met the owner, Melba Brajkovich. Melba comes to Wine Shows in New York City almost every year. Gladys invited us to come to her home for a light dinner after we toured the winery. We happily accepted. Her husband, Ron, came back to guide us to their home. Gladys had prepared hot dogs, bacon, poached eggs, put out cheese and crackers and three kinds of cookies. The food was great and their home was very lovely. Their home is about ¾ of a mile out of Kumeu on 50 acres of beautiful land. (Since we were there, their son and his family moved back from Auckland.) We left their home about 7 p.m. and headed for Hamilton. We got a nice two bedroom suite at The Barclay Motel. In addition to the two bedrooms and bath, the living room had two sofas that made beds plus a very nice kitchen and eating area. Pam and Joe went downstairs to the laundry and washed two loads of clothes, but due to the late hour decided to wait and dry them in the morning. Joe and Mike both seem to be taking colds. All to bed by 10:30

Friday, July 16 we had breakfast in our suite. Pam dried the clothes while we packed up. We drove from Hamilton to Rotorua in the rain. We stopped at a pharmacy and bought cold medicine for Joe and Mike. We drove around town and found a lovely restaurant where we had lunch. The name was "Triple Five Café". The food was wonderful, but never found out the meaning of the name. We got rooms (jj5311 & mkj5313) at The Millenium Hotel. Mike and family went to the spa while Joe and I took a nap. We made reservations for a Maori Dance program and dinner which was on the first level. After dinner, the dance group performed and one of the men enticed Mike to stand up and dance with them. Joe got it on video. We all laughed so much while Mike was "on stage" hamming it up.

Saturday, July 17 it had rained all night and the wind really blew. We went down to breakfast about 8:45. Afterward, we went to "The Kiwi Encounter". It is a new building for the purpose of a safe place to hatch Kiwi Eggs and build up the species. There was another walk-through park called "The Rainbow Springs". We didn't want to pay and walk in the rain to boot, so we just looked at their gift shop. We went back to the city park to see the Geysers and boiling pots. They were interesting, but the sulphur odor was very strong. We went to a beautiful museum and the building had originally been a bathhouse where people who could afford it, came to take hot mineral baths. (That was in the 1920s and 30s). They still had some of the original equipment in the small rooms for visitors to see. They showed us a movie about the bathhouse and some of the clients who came for their health. We went back to the hotel and the young Jurlinas went to the sauna again while Joe and I took a nap. Since it was raining so much we didn't get to do some things the children would have enjoyed. We dressed and went downtown to THE LONE STAR CAFÉ for dinner. The restaurant had several TVs and all were showing the playoff rugby game. Everyone wanted the All-Blacks to win which they did. Our food was wonderful. We went back to the hotel and to bed.

Sunday, July 18 we woke up to a sunny day. We went downtown to a wall climbing place where we spent about three hours because with all the rain we hadn't gotten to do much the children wanted to do. Mike and each member of his family had fun climbing. We spent about three hours there. We then had to go to Starbucks for coffee and went to McDonalds for a big mac. We left for Auckland and along the way took a side trip trying to find the location where Lord of the Rings was filmed. Obviously we turned the wrong way as we learned it was east of us. We got back on the main highway and suddenly Mike said, "Don't say anything as a policeman is telling me to stop". Sure enough he got a speeding ticket which he had to pay in Auckland the next morning. We had dinner near the airport and went back to the Holiday Inn to spend the night.

Monday, July 19 we had breakfast at Penny's restaurant just off the lobby. Then we loaded our packed bags into the car and got to the airport about 1:45 p.m. We checked our bags at Quantas. Then we went upstairs and looked at all the shops and bought some more gifts including 5th Ave. perfume for myself. Joe & I left the kids and went upstairs to the Quantas first class lounge. They had a lovely buffet set up for the passengers. Of course, we had lunch. A few minutes before loading time, we went downstairs and met up with the kids. We boarded the plane at 5:40 p.m. Shortly after takeoff we were told we could set our watches at 12:15 p.m. for Los Angeles time. We listened to BIG COUNTRY MUSIC radio station and also saw a rotten movie.

Tuesday, July 20 we were served breakfast about 9:25 a.m. We landed at LAX Airport about 10:45. Our flight for Dallas left at 3:30. The kids couldn't get on that flight and had to wait for a later one. We called Carol Ann and Bill and they met us at the airport in Dallas about 6:30. We ate dinner on the way home and got to bed about 12:30 a. m. We slept until about 2:30 p.m. the next day we were so tired. Victor Jurlina called us Wednesday night to make sure we had gotten home o.k.

www.ingramcontent.com/pod-product-compliance
Lightning Source LLC
Chambersburg PA
CBHW032003040426
42448CB00006B/476